Code Red

God's Plan for Humankind Throughout the Ages – Revealed!

P.P. Hallam

malcolm down
PUBLISHING

First published 2020 by Malcolm Down Publishing Ltd
www.malcolmdown.co.uk

24 23 22 21 20 7 6 5 4 3 2 1

British Library Cataloguing in Publication Data
A catalogue record for this book is available from the British Library.

ISBN 978-1-912863-59-4

Cover design by P.P. Hallam
Art direction by Sarah Grace

Endorsements

When I think of my friend Paul Hallam, I think of someone who is gripped with purpose and a God-given vision. I think of someone who is impassioned to impart God's heart and mind to the next generation. Not only is Paul a wonderful pastor and leader, but he is a father to the orphan, a mentor to the mentee and a supporter to those who lack much-needed encouragement. His life truly is a life of impact and significance.

I was therefore honoured when Paul asked me to read and endorse his new book, *Code Red.*

Code Red takes the reader on a biblical journey of fresh insight and thinking. To tell you the truth, it blew my mind!

Paul skilfully unwraps innovative thinking by unveiling the enemy's strategy to infiltrate the human condition. His desire being to create his own bloodline and lineage by corrupting man's 'seed'. Gripping stuff!

Paul the apostle encouraged the Church of Jesus Christ not to be ignorant of the enemy's devices (2 Corinthians 2:11), and Paul has done what was requested. Ignorance has been abolished! *Code Red* engages the reader with relevance, spiritual insight and practical expression. I highly recommend it.

Mark Stevens, Founder and leader, Rise Church, Leeds UK

A thoroughly researched, biblically based work that traces the spiritual forces at work from the dawn of creation through to their insidious influence on our contemporary spiritual climate. Provocative, challenging and controversial, it invites the reader to build a defence against their incursion into our own lives.

John Glass, chair of Council for the Evangelical Alliance, 2014, General Superintendent of Elim Pentecostal Church 1999-2016

In *Code Red*, Paul follows the redemption story from creation to the twenty-first century. This is a book infused with scripture, challenging us to discern the 'signs of the times'. This is one of the most thought-provoking books I've read in recent years. As Paul himself states, you may not agree with all his conclusions, but this well-researched book demands your serious consideration.
Dr Tim Tucker, CEO of The Message Trust, South Africa

In this timely book, my friend Paul Hallam brings non-religious, powerful and yes, prophetic teaching. It's a must-read, especially in days like these.
Andy Hawthorne, OBE, founder and CEO of The Message Trust, UK

In the medical world, 'code red' refers to a critical situation that needs immediate action and, in this book, Paul exposes the immediate action needed for our current situation where the world is crying out for 'normality'. So, get yourself ready for an inquisitive journey through theology, science, medicine, ancient history, and make sure you are ready to challenge your preconceptions. If in doubt, check the alternative sources and this will open a new world of understanding. Prepare yourself for a slow start, setting the scene, followed by a complex read to a great final finish which will change your life forever!
Professor Christian Hendriksz, CEO of FYMCA Medical Ltd, UK

Contents

Thank You

I would like to express my deepest gratitude and love to my wife, Mags, for her faithful support and love for well over three decades. For me to be the pastor, leader, author, entrepreneurial risk-taker and activist that I am, would never have been possible without her.

Thanks also to the amazing church congregation that I pastor, along with our incredible team at The Lighthouse Church in Manchester. I am humbly and deeply thankful.

Foreword

The times in which we live have witnessed a surge of interest as to where humankind is in the canvas of time. God, the architect of the ages, has graciously seen it fit to take us into His confidence concerning His plan for the future and has revealed it to us in His Word.

The Bible appears sometimes to be like a puzzle; we pick up the pieces and wonder which fits where. But what makes it easier is that God's Word is given to us as a template to see the whole picture.

In this book *Code Red*, P.P. Hallam has synthesized a whole plethora of questions into an easy-to-understand narrative of God's plan through the ages.

I prayerfully endorse this book to you and know it will bring greater clarity to the way you and I see events as they unfold. My dear friend and golfing buddy, Paul, has so succinctly and with such revelation knowledge given us insightful analysis to the *Code Red* plan of God.

May God our Father, who gave His Son – who by the shedding of His precious blood we were given salvation, and by whose second coming we will be received into glory, and by the indwelling of the Holy Spirit He will show us 'things to come' (John 16:13) – may the Lord our God be pleased to use this book for His glory!

Robert D'Roza
Pastor
Hope Chapel
Bangalore
India

Introduction

The most common question asked today is: 'If there's really a God, why is there so much suffering? Why do the innocent suffer so much, while the guilty, evil people get away with murder?'

The truth is, bad stuff happens to good people. And you know what? Good stuff happens to bad people too. It's the all-too familiar result of living on an imperfect planet.

This book has been written, not just to explain the injustice there is on this earth, or to just convince people there really is a God, but to show how things are playing out in a much bigger and more complex way than most people have ever realised. There is a much deeper and sometimes 'darker' side to the question of wickedness and evil in the world and I for one feel it's time we explained the unfolding and apocalyptic unveiling of the historic, prophetic, preordained will of Almighty God. This is what I have called 'Code Red' for reasons that will become clear as you read the book.

On the lead-up to Easter Week, we celebrate Palm Sunday. It's a day which is deeply prophetic, foretold in the Old Testament:

> Behold, your King is coming to you; He is just and having salvation, Lowly and riding on a donkey, A colt, the foal of a donkey.
> (Zechariah 9:9)

This was exactly fulfilled in Christ Jesus when he rode into Jerusalem. Matthew records this in his gospel:

> All this was done that it might be fulfilled which was spoken by the prophet [Zechariah], saying: … 'Behold, your King is

> coming to you, Lowly, and sitting on a donkey, A colt, the foal of a donkey.'
> (Matthew 21:4-5)

The crowd are jubilant and they all cry with one voice:

> Hosanna to the Son of David!
> 'Blessed is He who comes in the name of the LORD!'
> Hosanna in the highest!
> (Matthew 21:9)

Such was the excitement, the hopes and dreams of a nation, a people and tribe were placed in Him; however, all this hope and praise turned to hate and treachery in a matter of four days! Actually, only five days later, the same crowd, same faces, the very same people cried out for Jesus' death.

Pilate, therefore, willing to release Barabbas – who had been thrown into prison for a rebellion made in the city and for murder! – asks the people to decide who to release, Barabbas or Jesus?

> The crowd shouted … 'Crucify Him, crucify Him!'
> (Luke 23:21)

How have we gone from a triumphant entry into Jerusalem five days before, to a murderous mob who would rather crucify an innocent man who did good deeds everywhere he went, to choosing a murderer to live in His place? It's a shocker, to be honest.

What it does show is the fickleness of the human heart, and the deep wickedness that lies within each of us. Thankfully, this propensity for evil is subdued and constrained by our consciences and our moral values and the personal standards we have been taught and nurtured in. But what is clear and undeniable is that the heart is deceitfully wicked, 'above all things' says the prophet Jeremiah (Jeremiah 17:9).

Today, nothing has changed; we are still capable of awful atrocities against our fellow human beings. From the invasion of the Vikings to the Middle Ages and the Crusades of the so-called 'Holy Wars', all sides were guilty of horrific and heinous acts of cruelty to one another. Religion, it has been said many times, is responsible for the murder and even genocide of people, whole communities, whether it was the Spanish and Portuguese[1] in South America, the Conquistadors, the Incas and Aztecs virtually being wiped from the face of the earth (supposedly in the name of Christ and His Church!), or the Turks, massacring the Armenians,[2] razing their towns, villages and communities to the ground in the name of Islam. Stalin,[3] on the other hand, had no belief in God, but was responsible for murdering millions of people, including his own. He killed far more people than Hitler, whose god was power and white supremacy. Britain too was guilty and has blood on its hands by the bloody subjugation of nations such as those in Africa, India and many other far-off lands in its quest for power and worldwide supremacy.

So, what's the common denominator here? Despite the centuries, even millennia that have elapsed, one thing stands out from all others: our total inability to learn from our past. The reality is that the human condition (of the heart) is not getting better with time. Some would argue it is getting worse, much worse. Whilst our intelligence has grown almost exponentially over the past fifty years, the condition and state of our heart seems to have become 'darker' and much more evil.

1. www.discoveringbristol.org.uk (accessed 13.7.20).
2. www.nationalgeographic.com; www.history.com (accessed 13.7.20).
3. www.news.stanford.edu; www.history.com (accessed 13.7.20).

In the opening chapter, I aim to show beyond doubt, we are all journeying on a precipitous course, a downward spiral that will end in eventual catastrophe. Consequences will come that will affect the whole of humanity; the fact is, every individual will be personally affected by the things we are bringing upon ourselves. Note, God is not bringing them upon us; we are masters and architects for our own downfall. Our cleverness will also be our curse. This is not my 'conjecture' or 'mere speculation', it is my interpretation of the signs of the times and seasons Jesus Himself spoke of in Matthew 24, combined with the prophetic element of Holy Scripture.

1. Where Did it All Go Wrong?

Death is often a taboo subject here in the Western world. We don't really discuss it much. We don't investigate the reasons for it, the 'science' of our mortality. We do a lot to prevent it happening, though, and to stop its eventual, inevitable arrival in our lives. Despite that, the fact is, death is 100 per cent certain in our normal life cycle: 100 people out of 100 will die.

Yet, there is a reason for this downward trajectory of death. It lies in the fact that the ground was cursed, and that humanity is fallen, and subject to that curse.

I am an unapologetic creationist. With all my being, soul and spirit, I believe I was created, designed and put together by God. I have never believed in evolution as the origin of humankind. I don't believe in humanity being in existence for millions and billions of years. In the last fifty years, you can see the incredible advances we have made in technology, chemistry, medicine and science. We have the ability to destroy whole nations, communities, cities. None of the advances of science, physics and knowledge in itself is evil. The danger isn't in the discovery of all these things, but the danger is – guess where? Within humanity itself. The same humanity that discovers is the same humanity that has the capacity or the opportunity to use that knowledge for good or evil. Our amazing ability to discover new things can also be our demise, and lead to destruction. It's not the gun that kills, it's the person who pulls the trigger! It's not the bomb that devastates, it's the person who decides to press the button. It's not the car that kills, it's the driver. So, I could go on, and on.

Many things have been given to us, to discover and to use for our benefit and advantage, but we have misused gifts given to us. Sometimes we have misused what we have been given; other times we have abused what we have been given.

When we misuse what we have been given, we get a different result to what was initially intended. I bought some of our kids in India[4] a cricket set. They love cricket. We have several homes and look after many abandoned children and we continue to rescue many from the streets, some as young as four years of age.

Well, the cricket bats were used to play cricket, but they were also used as a hammer to smash wickets onto the ground. Guess what? The set didn't last twelve months! That's due to misuse. Now, if one of the lads hits another boy with a bat, that's abuse. A simple example to some, maybe, but this is happening all over the world right now on an alarming scale.

For example, take television. The invention of Mr Logie Baird was a fantastic invention. Amazing! Live pictures delivered to someone's home. OK, so those pictures in black and white looked like we had just had a snowstorm every day, outside and inside! Fast forward to the present TV set, HD, Ultra HD, plasma TV screens, but now, we see the grotesque violence, horror, pornography and dreadfully abusive stuff at the touch of a button. Violent, addictive games are creating one of the most devastating, disturbing and destructive experiences, threatening our children today. Tell me, please, is this still progress? Is this bringing an improvement in our daily lives? *Is it making us feel better in life?* Is it making our lives happier and more enjoyable? I suggest definitely not. If so, why are so many, gifted, talented, 'successful', famous, wealthy people living in depression and some even take their own lives?

Robin Williams made millions laugh. I personally thought he was one of the funniest people on the planet. Gone, in a moment. Gary Speed, the footballer and manager of Wales. Famous, talented, successful, family man. Gone! To put it simply, we are on a rapid

4. The church of which I am the pastor, The Lighthouse Church Manchester, has a charity called LIM (Lighthouse International Ministries). We have built children's homes and nearly one hundred churches in Africa and India, and a specialist children's centre in Romania. See www.limuk.org (accessed 29.7.20).

trajectory of death and decay. It's not just we who are dying, though, our planet is dying too. We are responsible for that as well. We are dying, slowly, but surely. We are suffocating on a cursed earth.

The law of entropy

The law of entropy makes it clear. Everything is in a state of moving towards decline, decay and eventually, death. Even young plants, animals, people. As soon as we come into the world, our days begin the countdown to death. This is summed up succinctly in the book of Isaiah.

> The voice said, 'Cry out!' And he said, 'What shall I cry?' 'All flesh is grass, And all its loveliness is like the flower of the field. The grass withers, the flower fades, Because the breath of the LORD blows upon it; Surely the people are grass. The grass withers, the flower fades, But the word of our God stands forever.'
> (Isaiah 40:6-8)

Here we see clearly written, some 2,700 years ago by the prophet Isaiah, the law of entropy as we know it scientifically today.

It's amazing that we agree with the first part of the message, but not with the second part: 'The word of our God stands forever.'

Yet I believe, along with many, that the Bible – the Scriptures, New Testament and Old, the sixty-six books of the Bible, canonised by our ancestors long before TV and social media come into being, with more than 30,000 ancient manuscripts to evidence its authenticity – is God's revealed word to the whole of humanity. In short, I believe in both statements:

1. The grass withers, the flower fades … (or dies)
2. The word of our God stands forever.

Let me say very clearly, I am not a religious person. I refer very strongly to this in my first book *The Rubicon*[5] that shares the story of my life, and my call into ministry and that of The Lighthouse Church and charity, which has grown beyond many people's expectation.

I believe God is for us, not against us! I believe He is wholly, totally positive in His approach and intention to us, His creation. When God made us, He did not create us as flawed human beings – many argue that if He created us, He created something with a fault in design, but when He created us, He created us with one of the most powerful things ever, *the power to choose*, i.e. free will. God had no intention of creating robots (it seems He left that to us to do). This was not a design flaw, it was a 'design feature' – the angels were created with this feature too. Just shows how important free will is to God.

This 'design feature' is both good and bad, depending on how it is used! Now, maybe you'll begin to see where we are going. Choice is a huge thing; it is massive. Our choices in life are what makes us – or ultimately breaks us. God wants us to choose Him. To not only acknowledge Him, but actually *worship Him*, but not by force, or coercion, but by choosing to. This is more important to God than can possibly be imagined! The Bible also tells us that this era of choice and free will is actually not going to last forever. We are told:

> at the name of Jesus *every* knee should bow … and … *every* tongue should confess that Jesus Christ is Lord, to the glory of God the Father.
> (Philippians 2:10-11, my italics)

5. Paul Hallam, *The Rubicon* (Camarillo, CA: Xulon Press, 2014).

2. Boundaries

I enjoy playing golf. Some people obviously don't, but I love it. It gives me a chance to compete, test my character, determination and skill against others, or more importantly, the course. The aim is to get 'pars' or even 'birdies' (one below par). Whilst playing this tough but very challenging game, one must always be aware of the 'boundaries'. The game can only be enjoyed within the boundaries. If you hit your ball off the course, beyond the boundaries, guess what? It's a penalty! You have to go back and play the shot again with a shot penalty.

Likewise, if you go 'OOB' (out of bounds), there are consequences. There are certain holes where you have white posts denoting a boundary. If you go out of the boundary you will also have to play the shot again, returning to the exact same spot, again with a shot dropped. It can be a very frustrating game. But suppose we said, 'You know what? Let's get rid of all the out of bounds areas. In fact, let's make sure there is no water to hit over – or into! Let's even go a step further, let's have no penalties for going astray or hitting an errant shot. After all, we make mistakes. Let's also get rid of those pesky bunkers. They can be a nightmare and a card wrecker.

If we got rid of all these aspects of the game, we would end up with a sport that is pretty meaningless, rewards bad play and poor shots instead of rewarding skilful play, and improving performance. Our game, in fact, would not improve, but deteriorate. Why should it improve? There would be no challenge, no real fun and no rewards for great shots.

This is exactly what is happening in our world today, but on a much more serious level. We are busy moving the boundaries in life. Where? How? Well, I'm going to give you several examples. Firstly, let's start with schools teaching sport, but not letting anyone win for fear of someone being upset that they lost. Wow! How is that preparing kids for the realities and rigours of life? Other boundaries are far more damaging to society. The removal of the boundary of marriage being important, and distinctly and uniquely between a man and a woman. This is a boundary shift that is already causing a meltdown in society. It has also triggered other boundary removals. That of gender. People can now change their gender and get helped medically, surgically and psychologically to do it. Is this wrong? Is this right before God? I would answer in a different way altogether. Boundaries are primarily in place for three reasons:

1. To keep things out
2. To keep things in
3. To give notification of a line of demarcation

David Cameron, the former British Prime Minister, in his farewell speech, said that he believed introducing same-sex marriages (SSM) was one of his proudest achievements. Now, let me say emphatically, I have nothing against gay people, and those who are transgender, homosexual etc. People are people, and they make their choices based on many determining factors. But what I am saying is that there have always been boundaries. And boundaries have always been crossed and traversed. Some boundaries are good to cross, and the challenge of breaking a world record in the 100m sprint is a great thing. Breaking through the speed barrier is exciting. Manchester City broke the record for a number of goals scored, winning the English Premier League in 2017-18. These are boundaries worth breaking. Borders that are there to be crossed.

I often travel to Eastern Europe, to India and Africa. Every time, we fly across borders and boundaries. Gladly, when I fly, permission has already been granted for us to cross into someone else's airspace, otherwise there would be trouble – you get the picture? OK, so say

Russia says the Crimea boundary is something they don't agree with, and pours into Crimea, which basically happened in 2014 – Ukraine is not going to be too happy. Europe is not happy. The Second World War came about when Germany crossed the border into Poland, then France. To emphasise – borders are essential lines of demarcation. We need to know which borders to cross and which to steer clear of. Unfortunately, our political leaders have moved endless borders and boundaries socially, economically, religiously and psychologically.

Because of boundary shifts by the medical world, the most dangerous place to live in the world for a child is in its mother's womb. A Bible is banned in many schools, but welcomed in most prisons. A person can sleep with whoever they want at sixteen, but they can't vote. A person is free to have faith, but often not to share it or speak out about it. A chaplain can now be an atheist! A girl can have sex with someone, even if she's under age, and get the 'morning after' pill without anyone informing her parents. Whether you agree with me or not, I think you'll agree that the boundaries in our world are changing rapidly and irreversibly. You may think that's a good thing. I personally think it's a bad thing, that depends on our own opinions, but I think that there's been a large shift in the common boundaries of life.

This has always happened within individual's choices, by the way. The Roman emperor Nero married a young man who he took to be his 'wife'. There's certainly 'nothing new under the sun' (Ecclesiastes 1:9). I'm aware it will be not be popular with some, expressing what I believe to be a valid interpretation of the boundaries set by the Bible, God's Word. The trouble is, most people will say 'What is truth?' which was exactly the words of Pilate to Jesus, just before his crucifixion (John 18:38). There are very few 'absolutes' today, right is merging with wrong, wrong is 'subjective' to the point of muzzling anyone who would dare to stick their head above the parapet and say, 'This is *wrong*! This is out of bounds!' Irrespective of whether the Bible calls it out of bounds, people are falling over themselves to find ways around God's boundaries, these lines of demarcation. As the saying goes, 'Better a fence at the top of the cliff, than an ambulance at the bottom.'

So, back to our original point. I believe, rather than asking if something is right or wrong, let's start with the question, do we believe in boundaries? Are they good or bad? The systematic removal of boundaries is a sign of the times in which we live.

In my garden, I have a traditional wooden fence. It's there to show my neighbours where their property finishes and where mine begins. I am not responsible for what happens outside of the perimeter of my garden. I'm solely responsible for what happens inside. Occasionally, however, I may have to speak to my neighbour – for example, when their trees and bushes have grown over my shed roof. The weight virtually crushed the roof at one point (totally my own fault for not maintaining it on my side of the fence). In the end I demolished the large shed, and cut back my neighbour's offending foliage, because it had crossed his boundary and come into mine.

When things begin to affect us as Christians, I think we should speak out. I am not responsible for how others live. But I am responsible for my life. I also believe God has set boundaries that are helpful – they keep us focused. Others are there to keep others out. We definitely need God's wisdom to know which is which!

3. The Race to the Bottom

It seems a pretty negative title for our third chapter, but it's essential for us to understand 'why' we are living in such a mixed-up world.

From the beginning of creation, since the fall of humankind, there has been a 'race to the bottom' caused by a gradual decline in the relationship we have with our Creator. With this has come an inner deterioration and the constant degrading of our lives from a spiritual point of view.

The Bible says that God created the original couple who gave birth to humankind, Adam and Eve – now, many scientists agree, we all come from one man and one woman, producing the necessary chromosomes for life.[6]

According to Genesis, God said *there's one thing you must not do* – 'of the tree of the knowledge of good and evil you shall not eat' (Genesis 2:17). What is the one thing they did? You guessed it! They ate from the forbidden fruit. Tempted and seduced by the fallen archangel Lucifer, now known as Satan, they ate of the tree of the knowledge of good and evil (remember what we said in the previous chapter about boundaries?).

I find it fascinating that ancient languages confirm the Genesis account. A whole chapter in this book is devoted to looking at 'the Code' in language, so we will come back to this topic later.

God warned the couple, 'in the day that you eat of it you shall surely die' (Genesis 2:17). Amazingly, they both ate – incidentally, because the two had become one flesh through physical intimacy of sexual intercourse, and one emotionally and psychologically. When

6. See www.nypost.com; www.ancient-origins-net; article published 24 November 2018, Mail online. www.dailymail.co.uk (accessed 13.7.20).

Eve saw the fruit looked good, and ate, there was no initial effect. Only when Adam had eaten the fruit were their eyes opened together and they both realised they were naked and were ashamed of their nakedness. So much so they sewed clothes from fig leaves, and hid themselves, like naughty children from their Creator and Father, Almighty God.

It's also interesting here, how God had created the tree of the knowledge of good and evil before He had created Adam and Eve. In other words, the ability to choose was in place before those who could choose were created. The Genesis record says trees were created on the third day, Genesis 1:11, and we know Adam and Eve were created on the sixth day. If you don't hold a literal interpretation of the Bible, and I know many do not, stick with me here for a bit. We know from the biblical record that Adam and Eve crossed the line, crossed the boundary God had set, and the day they ate they survived. They didn't actually die like God had said. Some people say, 'See, God did not fulfil His own rule here.' But now we come to an enormous point of revelation. While it is true, they did not die physically, they died spiritually and they became separated from Eden, God's place of perfection; paradise was lost once and for all – or was it?

'Death' in the original Genesis account, traditionally believed to be written by Moses, in the Hebrew language, actually meant 'separation'. It does not mean final breath or execution, or the extinguishing of life.

> in the day that you eat … you shall surely die ...
> (Genesis 2:17)

The moment Adam and Eve's transgression came into the open, God did four things:

1: He cursed the ground (Genesis 3:17).
2: He 'made tunics of skin, and clothed them' (Genesis 3:21).
3: He expelled them from the Garden of Eden (Genesis 3:23).
4: He placed a cherubim with a flaming sword at the east (entrance) 'which turned every way, to guard the way to the tree of life' (Genesis 3:34).

The first point in particular is highly significant. Everything that follows relates to the ground. The animal skins, the garden itself, the very tree of life was growing out of the ground. Let's go back further before we go ahead. Man was made from what? The dust of the earth is the soil, the ground! How amazing that although God did not curse the man or the woman, His creation, He cursed the very thing they were created from, and the very thing they would live from, the ground. He explains very clearly why, later on, to Adam and Eve and their two sons. Cain and Abel brought offerings to God; one was acceptable, the other offensive and unacceptable. Note that God had covered the couple's nakedness with animal skins. That means that He got them to remove their home-made fig-leaf coverings. They too originated from the ground; as such they were not acceptable as coverings for their nakedness. Only the skin of an animal would suffice. Therefore, we must conclude that the first animal that was killed, was killed by God himself, and that it was not killed for meat but for a covering. This means God set a whole, brand-new precedent. That of 'covering' our nakedness – shame, i.e. the record of wrongdoing (sin) and disobedience, killing an innocent animal in the process, meaning something living and breathing had to die in order to cover the ancestors of the living!

In cursing the ground, God is specific in His judgement:

Curse on the soil:

> Cursed is the ground for your sake;
> In toil you shall eat of it
> All the days of your life.
> Both thorns and thistles it shall bring forth for you,
> And you shall eat the herb of the field.
> In the sweat of your face you shall eat bread
> Till you return to the ground,
> For out of it you were taken;
> For dust you are,
> And to dust you shall return.
> (Genesis 3:17-19)

So, in verse 23 we read, 'therefore the LORD God sent him out of the garden of Eden to till the ground from which he was taken'.

Curse on the serpent:
God also cursed the serpent who deceived the woman.

> So the LORD God said to the serpent:
> 'Because you have done this,
> You *are* cursed more than all cattle,
> And more than every beast of the field;
> On your belly you shall go,
> And you shall eat dust
> All the days of your life.
> (Genesis 3:14)

Verse 15 continues:

> And I will put enmity
> Between you and the woman,
> And between your seed and her Seed;
> He shall bruise your head,
> And you shall bruise His heel.'

Prophecy over the Seed of the woman:

> To the woman He said:
> 'I will greatly multiply your sorrow and your conception;
> In pain you shall bring forth children;
> Your desire shall be for your husband,
> And he shall rule over you.'
> (Genesis 3:16)

It's interesting how 'the curse' came in. First, God curses the serpent; second, God addresses the woman (no mention of it being a curse); third, God curses the ground.

Again, it is interesting that the curse on the serpent has a special element to it. It would crawl on its belly and eat dust.

Even today the snake strikes fear into many people. In Africa, India, Australia and South America snakes can be exceptionally dangerous. Often in my travels to India, I have encountered snakes, mostly cobras, some grass snakes or kraits. There is a particularly dangerous one in the jungle areas I often visit called 'Russell's viper'. It is deadly. Mostly because it is found in the most obvious of places, sleeping in-between rocks, small stones and leaves. The problem also is magnified by the fact that many agricultural workers in the area wear hardly anything on their feet; stepping onto a lazy, sleeping Russell's viper can only mean one thing – death in a matter of minutes. Well over 45,000 people die every year of snake bites in India.[7] People are right to fear the most venomous of snakes, the black mamba of Africa, the spectacled cobra of Asia, or the brown snake of Australia, for example. Yet even so… was it really a talking snake that was responsible for the temptation of Eve and the subsequent fall of the whole human race?

Many people believe in God. Faith in God has been in existence since – guess what? The beginning of creation: not a surprise, I know! But there is far more belief in God than there is in 'the devil'. Many think such belief belongs in the Middle Ages, or perhaps the Dark Age. But the Bible makes it clear that Satan is real. He is an entity, plus he has third of the angelic host who are on his side.

It is clear that when God first created the heavenly host, i.e. angels, seraphim, cherubim and other celestial beings, that He did so with the freedom to choose. The prophets Isaiah and Ezekiel allude to the rebellion that took place in heaven, prior to the creation that took place upon the earth.

> How you are fallen from heaven,
> O Lucifer, son of the morning!
> How you are cut down to the ground,
> You who weakened the nations!
> (Isaiah 14:12)

In this passage of Scripture we are reading about someone who 'fell from heaven', i.e. an angelic being – not human. Isaiah goes on to give more information on his fall from heaven:

---

7. See www.deccanherald.com (accessed 4.7.20).

For you have said in your heart:
'I will ascend into heaven,
I will exalt my throne above the stars of God;
I will also sit on the mount of the congregation
On the farthest sides of the north;
I will ascend above the heights of the clouds,
I will be like the Most High.'
Yet you shall be brought down to Sheol,
To the lowest depths of the Pit.
(Isaiah 14:13-15)

There is no doubt who Isaiah could be referring to. The image is clear as is the characterisation of exactly what made him fall. Pride. Note the 'I wills' – five in two verses.

Back in Genesis 3:1, the serpent says: 'Has God indeed said, "You shall not eat of every tree of the garden"?'

The woman replies: 'We may eat the fruit of the trees of the garden; but of the fruit of the tree which is in the midst of the garden, God has said, "You shall not eat it, nor shall you touch it, lest you die"' (Genesis 3:2-3).

The serpent then says: 'You will not surely die. For God knows that in the day you eat of it your eyes will be opened, and you will be like God, knowing good and evil' (Genesis 3:4-5).

It is not difficult to see the similar tones of Lucifer here, in the quest to be 'like God': 'I will be like the Most High' (Isaiah 14:14).

Now, we need to look at a very interesting piece of scripture, Ezekiel 28:12-15. It appears to be an analogy, a parallel of Lucifer with the then king of Tyre.

You *were* the seal of perfection,
Full of wisdom and perfect in beauty.
You were in Eden, the garden of God;

Every precious stone *was* your covering:
The sardius, topaz, and diamond,
Beryl, onyx, and jasper,
Sapphire, turquoise, and emerald with gold.
The workmanship of your timbrels and pipes
Was prepared for you on the day you were created.
'You were the anointed cherub who covers;
I established you;
You were on the holy mountain of God;
You walked back and forth in the midst of fiery stones.
You *were* perfect in your ways from the day you were created,
Till iniquity was found in you.

The prophet then begins to speak in verses 16 and 17 of how God dealt with him:

you sinned;
Therefore I cast you as a profane thing
Out of the mountain of God;
And I destroyed you, O covering cherub …
I cast you to the ground …

Some of this is still very much in the future, as the Bible states clearly Satan is alive and at the moment has been unleashed upon the earth. Jesus Himself said in Luke 10:18: 'I saw Satan fall like lightning from heaven' and John the apostle also writes in the last book of the Bible: 'And I saw a star fallen from heaven to the earth. To him was given the key to the bottomless pit' (Revelation 9:1). The author of Revelation, John, writes:

> And war broke out in heaven: Michael and his angels fought with the dragon; and the dragon and his angels fought, but they did not prevail, nor was a place found for them in heaven any longer. So that great dragon was cast out, that serpent of old, called the Devil and Satan, who deceives the whole world; he was cast to the earth, and his angels were cast out with him.
> (Revelation 12:7-9)

Again in the book of Revelation:

> His [Satan, Lucifer, the devil] tail drew a third of the stars of heaven and threw them to the earth.
> (Revelation 12:4)

It is clear from the above that Lucifer, Satan, also known as the devil, was in Eden, and referred to it as *serpent.* I do not believe for one minute it was 'a serpent' that spoke to Eve in the Garden of Eden. I believe it was Lucifer entering into 'the snake' and so the snake today is to be both revered and reviled. Of course, there are many who state that originally the snake had legs, because since the curse it was legless; maybe, maybe not, but that's not the purpose or aim of this book. My purpose in writing is to show the reader there is a narrative being played out and it began in Eden.

So, the ground was cursed, Adam and Eve are banished from the garden. The garden is secured by the cherubim guarding the entrance to the east. Now a totally new narrative begins. A whole new world is about to unfold. Things will never be exactly the same again. The curse on the ground will go on to affect every person who comes into the world from here on in.

4. The Seed of The Woman

Immediately after reading that Adam and his wife, Eve, are banished from the garden, we read that this triggered the beginning of so many problems. The first two sons, siblings, procreated, also have a test in which to choose between good and evil, right and wrong. We read Cain and then Abel were born to Adam and Eve. Abel, a shepherd, and Cain, who tilled the ground (Genesis 4:2).

We read that Cain and Abel brought offerings unto the Lord. 'Cain brought an offering of the fruit of the ground' (Genesis 4:3) and Abel 'brought ... the firstborn of his flock' (Genesis 4:4). But the Lord 'did not respect Cain and his offering' (Genesis 4:5). God tells Cain: 'If you do well, will you not be accepted? And if you do not do well, sin lies at the door. And its desire is for you, but you should rule over it' (Genesis 4:6-7).

Cain goes on to have a heated argument with his brother Abel in the field. Cain murders his brother through anger and jealousy. The first account of physical death and murder.

Firstly, let's turn to what happens with the offerings. Why one was accepted and the other rejected. It is to do with bringing a living sacrifice – a lamb – compared to bringing a sacrifice which is not an animal and of the ground. Remember, God had cursed the ground, so the fruit of his labours had an element of the curse upon it, i.e. it was unacceptable! God pointed it out and told Cain to try again! He could probably have got a lamb from his brother, but I guess pride stopped him and he paid the ultimate price.

Again, God infers how important life with the blood is: 'The voice of your brother's blood cries out to Me from the ground' (Genesis 4:10). God then, for the first time, curses a person – Cain – in Genesis 4:11.

The curse was going to make him unfruitful.
It was going to make him a fugitive.
It was going to make him a vagabond.
God also put a mark on Cain to protect him being killed in turn.
(Genesis 4:15)

Here we have lots of 'firsts' springing up in humankind:

- The first murderer
- The first man to be cursed by God
- The first son fallen after his father, Adam
- The first person to receive a mark from God
- The first to give birth after his generation
- The first to build a city (Genesis 4:17)

We then hear that Lamech – Cain's great-great-great grandson – also became a murderer (Genesis 4:23).

So, we see, it begins and it escalates. Sin is being passed from generation to generation. From Eden until now, all of humankind is subjected to the effects of the curse. Note, I did not say humankind is cursed. Remember, God did not curse the man or woman generally, but the ground and the serpent and Cain specifically.

Because God cursed the ground, it has had a very deep impact upon humanity. 'The earth' is a term used for the soil. Therefore, everything that issues from the ground is affected. Everything 'terrestrial' from the moment on is under the curse. We also see Adam and Eve, the results of the curse upon their sons Cain and Abel, Cain becomes the first murder and Abel becomes the first person murdered and the first person to die physically. Isn't it amazing that the first person ever to die physically did not die what we call a 'natural death'?

He died a premature death, which was directly related to sin, i.e. transgression – Cain's anger and jealousy with his brother and his offering. Not only this, but Adam and Eve's descendent Lamech also becomes a murderer. The second record of death in the Bible is also premature and due to anger. Lamech's defence for his action was that it was self-defence: 'I have killed a man for wounding me, Even a young man for hurting me' (Genesis 4:23). So we see sin and its effects passing down through the generations and its effects passing down through the genealogies.

We are told that Adam, the first man, lived to about 930 years old. I know many do not believe these numbers are correct; personally, I do, and I think it makes sense that in the early days of creation, when humanity was not supposed to die at all, that they would initially live for a very long time as the effects of sin, which ultimately is the reason for death (natural or otherwise), played out slowly in its cause and effect in the body. Paul the apostle, in his writing to the Romans, explains: 'Therefore, just as through one man sin entered the world, and death through sin, and thus death spread to all men, because all sinned' (Romans 5:12). He goes on to say in Romans 5:14: 'death reigned from Adam to Moses, even over those who had not sinned according to the likeness of the transgression of Adam…'

'The transgression of Adam', as Paul puts it, was specific, and it was clear. Paul makes it plain that the effects of it passed down to us all. This is extremely important to understand; Paul's talking about the condition of fallenness or sin, and not the specific sin itself. For instance, you and I were not in the Garden of Eden. You and I did not partake of the same fruit, but unfortunately, the consequences of that action have passed down to us via the inherent seed of man.

It is important also to note the only sinless man ever to have lived was Jesus Christ. That was made possible only by being born of a virgin, a woman, i.e. by bypassing the 'seed of man'. The Bible refers to Christ as the 'seed of the woman', not the seed of man. It's truly 'All About Eve'! In Genesis 3, the prophecy of Eve was very precise. Here is one of the first prophecies of the battle between Satan and the Seed of the woman. On the surface, the seed of the woman may be interpreted as plural, but the prophecy is clearly written as singular. 'He shall bruise your head', other versions read 'he will crush your head' (NIV) or 'strike' (e.g. NRSV). The emphasis, however, is on the head, not the heel, i.e. a blow to the head is far more damaging than a blow to the heel.

Many Bible scholars believe the seed of the woman to be 'Christ Jesus' who, says Matthew 1:21, is called 'Jesus', the Greek form of Joshua, because he will 'save his people from their sins'. The word/name 'Jesus' means 'the Lord saves'.

These verses from Genesis reveal the ongoing conflict that continues until this present day. The whole of humankind has been plunged into a dark, spiritual and sophisticated, complex war; no one can be neutral within the struggle, even though they may think they are, or even state they are. We see the war from the expulsion of the first couple in the Garden of Eden, throughout the atrocities of the plan to slay of the firstborn of the Hebrew males whilst in Egypt as captives (Exodus 1:15-16), to the genocide of Herod murdering all the male children of two years and under, from the time he heard of Jesus' birth from the Magi (Matthew 2:16-18). This infanticide was carried out to prevent the advent of the saviour – Moses in Egypt, and Christ for the world!

In Matthew 2:13 we witness another episode in the depths of human depravity. A puppet of the Roman Empire, Herod the Great was cunning and ruthless. He executed two of his wives and three of his sons who he suspected were conspirators to oust him from his throne.[8] Once he heard of Jesus' birth, who was called 'King of the Jews' by the Magi, he raged against the very idea of this new infant

8. Numbers vary; sources differ.

king. His murderous response is quite fascinating. He murders any male children in order to secure his own position as 'King of Jews' but a much deeper, darker and sinister battle is being played out. Jesus, the Seed of the woman in the very truest sense – not born of man, but the woman, a virgin, had to be killed, not for political, selfish reasons, but for deeper, spiritual, prophetic reasons. The Seed of the woman would bruise/crush/strike the serpent, Satan's head. Kill the infant Jesus and it would stop the prophecy in its tracks!

This leads me right into Code Red territory. The real reason for barbaric, cruel behaviour. It's not always obvious! As I often say, there's usually another reason behind the reason, beyond the reason given. It's called politics, and political intrigue ensues. The spirit world of fallen angels and demonic activity here, now, on earth is playing out under our noses – mostly unrecognised and undiscerned for what it truly is. The battle is for the souls, hearts and minds of humankind, including – yes, you've guessed it – yours and mine, and it is raging!

From Eden's banishment until this present day, we are all subject to the consequences of Adam and Eve's transgression. No one is beyond its reach and immune from its influence. It is through the curse we get tired, grow old and eventually die. Under the curse, murder still happens, though on a much larger and wider scale. Sickness, disease, war, famine, pain, sorrow, depression, loneliness, addiction are all either directly or indirectly caused by the cursing of the ground harking back to the transgression, the disobedience of the very first couple.

So, is there any hope? Is there any good news? Is there a way out of the curse? The answer is a definite 'yes' but as a huge, far-reaching decision initially plunged us into cursing and chaos, another huge, far-reaching decision can bring us out of the curse, its grip, its effects and its sense of hopelessness. This decision has to be deliberate, measured and sincere in order to lift us out of the darkness that engulfs our lives.

5. A Global Catastrophe

Before we fast forward to our present day, it is essential to understand more about how we came to where we are today.

The earth being cursed was to become so full of darkness and wickedness that something drastic would take place. Genesis 6 is perhaps the trigger point or main reason why God had no choice but to destroy the world. Fallen 'angels' also referred to in the Septuagint (the earliest entire manuscript of the Old Testament) as 'sons of God' came down to earth and were attracted to 'the daughters of men', seeing them as 'beautiful' (Genesis 6:2). They had sexual intercourse with these women who went on to give birth to half-human, half-angelic flesh: 'The Nephilim' (literally: giants). This was no coincidental occurrence. It was a strategic, calculated plan to stop the birth of the Messiah (the Saviour, Jesus) by polluting the human bloodline, through which Christ, the Son of God would be born of a virgin. Verse 3 continues:

> And the LORD said, 'My Spirit shall not strive with man forever, for he *is* indeed flesh; yet his days shall be one hundred and twenty years.' There were giants on the earth in those days, and also afterward, when the sons of God came in to the daughters of men and they bore *children* to them. Those *were* the mighty men who *were* of old, men of renown.
>
> Then the LORD saw that the wickedness of man was great in the earth, and that every intent of the thoughts of his heart was only evil continually. And the LORD was sorry that He had made man on the earth, and He was grieved in His heart. So the LORD said, 'I will destroy man whom I have created from the face of the earth, both man and beast, creeping thing and birds of the air, for I am sorry that I have made them.' But Noah found grace in the eyes of the LORD.
>
> (Genesis 6:3-8)

I have covered the subject of 'the Nephilim' in some detail further on in this book, so let us return to the most destructive event in our world, as far as humankind is concerned.

The Bible teaches us that this was an enormous, worldwide catastrophe. A flood that covered the whole known world, its human inhabitants, animals and creeping things. It was designed to destroy all the inhabitants corrupted by the new, 'strange flesh' (Jude 1:7). The seed of Satan.

The story of Noah's ark is often regarded as nothing more than a children's story nowadays. My wife had a beautiful pop-up book with the complete story of God rescuing Noah and his family and the animals in a huge wooden boat called an ark! Laugh as we may concerning this story, but start to dig into what the Bible says happened and it may surprise you that there is an increasingly overwhelming amount of belief in a catastrophic event that wiped out a large amount of fauna and flora in a pretty short space of time.

For example, the biblical record of the flood records things of great interest.

1. Before the flood there was no rain (Genesis 2:5-6). The earth was watered by dew from the earth, mists rising from the ground.
2. There would have been a large population on the earth given the fact that people lived longer – up to nearly 1,000 years old. (I'm a literalist when it comes to numbers in the Bible when context does not support any other interpretation.)
3. There was a very large canopy of water above all the earth – a 'vapor', according to the Amplified Version, or 'mist' (KJV).
4. Because of the above, the world would have been very different than today. The climate would have been a temperature not too hot and not too cold. The overhead water canopy would have provided a biodiverse atmosphere in which many plants and

animals would grow much larger than at present. Life spans would be much higher in such a clement climate. Bodies are known to heal faster in such an environment when it is recreated. Even today we have tapped into using bio-spherical environments to increase the rapidity of natural healing.[9] The water canopy provided a protection from harmful rays to the skin and harmful gases. No radiation or anything that would be harmful to humankind was present in those early days of humankind.

5. There would be no precipitation, i.e. storms and violent weather conditions. There would not have been the volatile weather patterns we see today. Ozone depletion would not have existed and the weather would have been neutral across the planet. This is, of course, pre-Ice Age, if one takes a biblical view.
6. There would have been one single land mass. As yet the land had not been divided. These details are borne out through geographical and meteorological observations.[10] Even the shape of the existing coastlines, despite obvious erosion in many parts, still shows similar shapes and patterns to corresponding lands adjacent to them, only now separated by large tracts of water through seas and other water courses.
7. There were no seasons like now. These came into being post-flood after the sign of God's covenant to humankind in the form of a rainbow (Genesis 9:13). This was given as a promise by God that He would never destroy the earth by floodwater ever again.

According to Genesis, God instructed Noah to build this huge boat because He was going to wipe out the human race and start again! He found a man who was upright, honest and someone who had faith

9. So is it www.unesco-mab.org.uk (accessed 13.7.20).
10. This is called by some experts 'The Pangaea', a single massive continent. See www.livescience.com and www.nationalgeographic.com (accessed 23.2.18).

in God. There were others too, but these would die before God sent this great flood. It's important to note whilst Noah was building the ark – 120 years – no one had ever seen 'rain'.

It would take up to 120 years to build the boat we now refer to as Noah's ark. The description of a 'boat' is very poor, by the way, 'ark' is much more in keeping with the biblical imagery. The ark is similar in its concept to what baby Moses was found in when Pharaoh's daughter pulled him from the Nile. The ark was not built to sail across the oceans – it had no rudder. It was simply built to be unsinkable. It was built to float, and to drift. It had no anchor, either. It did, however, have a small window and 'one door'. There was only one way in and one way out. And that in itself is an image of salvation, which the scripture teaches is in none other than in Jesus Christ, 'the way, the truth, and the life' (John 14:6).

The ark is a type of Christ, who came to make a totally new creation. One that is within our lives and of the heart, not of the physical earth. This explains the similarities between Genesis 1 and John 1:

> In the beginning God created the heavens and the earth.
> (Genesis 1:1)

> In the beginning was the Word, and the Word was with God, and the Word was God.
> (John 1:1)

The length of time building the ark must have been a great test for Noah. All the time he was building it, the Bible says he was ignored.[11] Imagine building this thing by hand on dry land, miles away from any water! It also had three storeys. Before God sent the deluge, He told Noah that within seven days He would send the flood. He gave him

---

11. As implied in 2 Peter 2:5.

a week to prepare everything, food-wise, animal-wise and of course, there was time to say goodbye to all those who ignored his message. Then at the end of that week, boom! – it came – 'the fountains of the great deep' (Genesis 7:11) were opened up and the water canopy came down. Such was the precipitation that it rained for forty days and forty nights; combined with the opening of the fountains of the deep, the earth's floodwaters arose so much, they cleared the largest mountain peak by 25 and 40ft depending upon which cubit measurement is used (there are several). The waters prevailed for 150 days. That is, they 'rose' for five months! Mt Ararat in Turkey is where the ark came to rest in the middle of the seventh month; some Armenian people believe it has been discovered there. You may wish to research this for yourself. Mt Ararat is around 17,000ft above sea level, but it took another two and a half months before the tops of the mountains could be seen. It was more than an entire year aboard before the ark's inhabitants could disembark.

As you can imagine, such a flood, if it truly did happen, there would still be lots of evidence for it today. Guess what? There is. So much evidence, it will probably shock you.

Jesus, when referring to the flood in the New Testament, uses the word '*kataklumsmos*'[12] from which we get our word 'catastrophe': 'For as in the days before the flood (*kataklusmos*), they were eating and drinking, marrying and giving in marriage, until the day that Noah entered the ark, and did not know until the flood (*kataklusmos*) came and it took the all away, so also will the coming of the Son of Man be' (Matthew 24:38-39 – see also Luke 17:27). In regard to Peter's writings too, 2 Peter 2:5 says: 'and did not spare the ancient world, but saved Noah, one of eight people, a preacher of righteousness, bringing in the flood (*kataklusmos*) on the world of the ungodly ...'

---

12. See also 'kataklusmos', www.biblehub.com (accessed 4.7.20).

So we see Jesus and Peter refer to the 'the flood' as a '*katalusmos*' – a 'catastrophe' in which the whole world, apart from Noah, his wife, his three sons, Shem, Ham and Japheth and their wives, perished.

Despite this, the curse, its effects upon the earth, its animals, flora and fauna and all of humankind continued, until this present day. Furthermore, it should be noted that the world will no longer be flooded in such a way as described earlier. God gave the sign of a rainbow to us as a visible sign whenever it rains to remind us that this is temporary and not catastrophic, though we know heavy rain still can cause massive loss of life in the form of local devastation. This does not mean that there will not be terrible floods, tsunamis and so on on the earth. We know the weather patterns are becoming increasingly volatile these days and it appears that is set to continue, especially in what the Bible refers to as 'the last days' (2 Timothy 3:1), a term given to the last few years of the present age, or epoch. The evidence all around us shows we are living in this time. Global warming, earthquakes, natural disasters worldwide and news of wars are the human reason for the 'sorrows' Jesus talked about in his message to His disciples shortly before His crucifixion, whilst He gathered with them on the Mount of Olives (Matthew 24:3-14). Jesus then goes on to make this astonishing claim:

> For then there will be great tribulation, such as has not been since the beginning of the world until this time, no, nor ever shall be. And unless those days were shortened, no flesh would be saved; but for the elect's sake those days will be shortened. 'Then if anyone says to you, 'Look, here *is* the Christ!' or 'There!' do not believe *it*. For false christs and false prophets will rise and show great signs and wonders to deceive, if possible, even the elect. See, I have told you beforehand. Therefore if they say to you, 'Look, He is in the desert!' do not go out; *or* 'Look, *He*

> *is* in the inner rooms!' do not believe *it*. For as the lightning comes from the east and flashes to the west, so also will the coming of the Son of Man be.
> (Matthew 24:21-27)

Whilst there will always be science behind why the rainbow appears, why certain phenomena appear from time to time, there's also a biblical and prophetic side to these events too. That's what we miss, when we don't understand the code. The code still applies and its relevance has never been more clearly seen than in our day.

So the flood (*kataklusmos*) has shaped our world, our planet, our earth. As already described, the pre-flood world was a very different one than it is today. Going back even further, before the curse, the world was beautiful, pure, literally a paradise (Eden). The world to us as humankind was Eden. No one was initially outside of the garden until the fall so that was our world. An idyll which somehow remains a distant memory written as the utopia many of us secretly crave here on earth. Unfortunately, it does not exist on earth anywhere humanity is. If it did, we would destroy its perfect nature within a very short space of time. The trouble with the world is *us*! Humankind. The only good thing is, it's not the end. God has a plan of complete restoration and redemption. That's Code Red and you will begin to see how it all makes sense, but we are heading for the final countdown that God has prepared for the end of age.

6. The Nephilim

If I was in the film industry, and in the position to make a blockbuster movie, then this would be it. I'm still stunned that Mr Spielberg hasn't latched onto what would be a spine-tingling, nerve-wracking epic of a film. The script is basically all done for him!

Before I totally get stuck into this topic, I'd like to admit, some of what I'm about to put forward seems really far-fetched, especially if you're not an avid student of the Bible. To many people, the Bible is only an interesting, dusty historical book. A very complex and voluminous book. It's old (well over 2,700 years in parts). Because it's old, many see it as irrelevant, boring, and well, not really worth bothering much about. I'd say that pretty much sums up people's opinions these days. Because of that broad and sweeping opinion, this chapter is going to sound like a mixture of *Alien*, *Predator* and *The Da Vinci Code*! So get yourself ready – get prepared in your mind. This is not fantasy. This is for real and it's affecting everybody who has ever lived and will live out the rest of their lives here in this world.

Have you ever wondered how the Egyptians had the knowledge to build the pyramids, perform medical operations, gain such a knowledge of the so-called gods? How did they gain incredible astronomical knowledge and have such an emphasis on the afterlife? Have you ever asked, 'What's all this Greek mythology all about, with the gods and demi-gods Zeus, Perseus, Hercules, Achilles and the Titans?' The Roman gods and goddesses, and the Norse gods, Odin, Thor, Freya, and Stonehenge, UFOs and aliens? We have always been inquisitive about these myths and legends.

The answers to these questions and more, may be found in the book many people think is irrelevant, archaic and too voluminous to contemplate reading. Through its accounts of our history, our genealogies, our roots, to be precise, and yes, our origins, there are some profound and fascinating pointers to where all of this 'mythology' and 'folklore' came from. It's hardly surprising that if the Bible claims to be written about life from the beginning of creation until now, that there would be some reference to all the above. Well, folks – here it is! I give to you: the Nephilim.

In Genesis 6:1-4 we read:

> Now it came to pass, when men began to multiply on the face of the earth, and daughters were born to them, that the sons of God saw the daughters of men, that they were beautiful; and they took wives for themselves of all whom they chose. And the LORD said, 'My Spirit shall not strive with man forever, for he is indeed flesh; yet his days shall be one hundred and twenty years.' There were *giants* on the earth in those days, and also afterward, when the sons of God came in to the daughters of men and they bore children to them. Those were the mighty men who were of old, men of renown.
> (my italics)

The writer here is referring to the most sinister, evil and calculated attack on the human race that had ever been attempted. Churches, pastors and religious leaders have wrestled with these verses for hundreds of years. Unfortunately, we've been too afraid to teach this and share it with the people in and outside of the Church.

'The sons of God' are often translated as supernatural beings or angels.[13] The truth is that these are 'Elohim', gods (plural) in the Hebrew language. Their identity is also seen in the oldest book of the Bible, where God talks to Job about creation:

13. See CEB, CEV versions, for example.

> Where were you when I laid the foundations of the earth? ...
> When the morning stars sang together,
> And all the sons of God shouted for joy?
> (Job 38:4-7)

We can quite clearly see these 'sons of God' at the dawn of creation. The 'sons of God' are written as 'Elohim' i.e. gods. It is clear that these are a very significant group of celestial beings in their own right. Probably angelic beings of the highest order. It is some of these that Genesis refers to, who came down and sinned by having sexual intercourse with women, thereby mixing celestial flesh with terrestrial flesh, angelic bodies with human bodies, so that what was birthed was a physical hybrid capable of superhuman potential. These offspring became known as the Nephilim, 'mighty men ... of renown' also referred to as 'giants'.

Some past church leaders and students do not accept this position but believe the scripture merely refers to 'mighty men'. This, however, makes absolutely no sense when trying to interpret the Scriptures by cross-referencing them. Clearly the visitation has had an incredible effect on the world and its inhabitants. Furthermore, Jude 6 in the New Testament corroborates this line of interpretation: 'And the angels which kept not their first estate, but left their own habitation, [God] hath reserved in everlasting chains under darkness unto the judgment of the great day' (KJV).

These are none other than the fallen angels who Jude says forsook their habitation. They openly rebelled against God. This was the strategy of Satan, 'the serpent', to infiltrate the bloodline of Christ, thus preventing the coming of the Messiah. Satan knew from the prophecy in Eden that his head (the serpent's head) would be bruised by the Seed of the woman; that Someone would come who would overthrow him. Here it is in full view! The serpent's attempt to stop the coming Seed. From now on, he would stop at nothing to destroy the messianic bloodline. He knew if he could contaminate the genes of the human race by mixing 'strange flesh', all would be lost for humanity. He would then come in to save and get everyone to worship him in wickedness and evil.

This 'new race' was started before the flood at the time when humankind 'began to multiply on the face of the earth' (Genesis 6:1). The new beings, half-human and half-angelic, had great power (they were giants), but they had great wisdom too. No doubt these offspring of angels were taught great secrets by their fathers, the 'sons of God'. Following this verse of scripture, we see examples of men working with iron, being able to work metals and forge weaponry that would cause death and pain. In the lead-up to God flooding the earth, Scripture talks of a time of great violence and wickedness. How many Nephilim there were, we cannot really know, but there would have been many, because it grieved God so much that He caused this great flood to destroy them all. Only Noah, who had stayed true to God, and his wife, sons and their wives would be spared. They would be the chosen ones to start again in a new earth.

Some might ask, how is it possible for angelic beings to impregnate women here on earth? How can spirits possibly do such a thing? After all, the Bible teaches that flesh gives birth to flesh and spirit to spirit (John 3:6).

The problem here is, we are not just talking 'spirit'. The reality is that angels seem to have a physical dimension to them as well as a spiritual dimension. We read, for instance, of many encounters of men with angels. The men who met them face to face did not even know they were angels at first. Examples of this are so many in the Bible – see for example Abraham at Mamre, Genesis 18:1-8. Three angels meet with Abraham. He doesn't realise at first they're angels. He brings them something to eat and drink they eat and drink then two of them proceed to Sodom to rescue Abraham's nephew Lot and his family. Incidentally, while they're there, wicked men try to get Lot to bring the two men out to have sex with them (Genesis 19:5).

Gideon, in Judges 6, whilst threshing wheat at the winepress, was visited by an angel. He had no idea it was an angel at first. It's pretty much unthinkable that Gideon would question the angel, as he does in verse 13, if he had known at the beginning of the conversation that this was an angel.

Jesus Himself, in His resurrected body, had a physicality about Him that was very obvious to those around Him. On one occasion He came and stood in the midst of His disciples, ten of them, Judas having taken his own life after his betrayal of Christ and Thomas just, well, being absent. Note: the doors were locked. How did He get in? The disciples hurriedly tell everyone and Thomas, who infamously states he will not believe unless he sees with his own eyes.

> And after eight days His disciples were again inside, and Thomas with them. Jesus came, the doors being shut, and stood in the midst, and said, 'Peace to you!' Then He said to Thomas, 'Reach your finger here, and look at My hands; and reach your hand here, and put it into My side. Do not be unbelieving, but believing.' And Thomas answered and said to Him, 'My Lord and my God!'
>
> (John 20:26-28)

Can you see? It's like 'Take Two'! The doors are locked again. This time Thomas is there. Jesus makes sure there's no getting away from it for Thomas. He makes him touch his wounds in his hands and his side. This is none other than what Paul writes about in his letter to the Corinthian Church:

> But someone will say, 'How are the dead raised up? And with what body do they come?' Foolish one, what you sow is not made alive unless it dies. And what you sow, you do not sow that body that shall be, but mere grain – perhaps wheat or some other grain. But God gives it a body as He pleases, and to each seed its own body. All flesh is not the same flesh, but there is one kind of flesh of men, another flesh of animals, another of fish, and another of birds. There are also celestial bodies and terrestrial bodies; but the glory of the celestial is one, and the glory of the terrestrial is another.
> (1 Corinthians 15:35-40)

Can you see the amazing truth Paul is setting forth here? Can you now begin to understand how the two forms of physical nature – one terrestrial, the other celestial, were fused together in Genesis 6? Angels with humans producing offspring of incredible strength, size and knowledge too.

> Terrestrial = earthbound and limited
> Celestial = not earthbound, unlimited

> Do not forget to entertain strangers, for by so doing some have unwittingly entertained angels.
> (Hebrews 13:2)

I think the little verse from Hebrews sums up the matter succinctly. Angels can evidently change their appearance at will and have what I'd term a 'flexible physicality'.

Now maybe we'll be able to understand why there are all the tales of mythological beings, superhuman, 'gods' fathering offspring, like Zeus, and tales of Atlantis, its king, Atlas, from which we get Atlantic

Ocean, and Atlas for a book of the maps of the world. According to Greek mythology, Atlantis was destroyed in a great flood because of the great wickedness that was taking place. Could this be linked into the Nephilim destroyed in the flood? Sounds pretty close to me!

Justin Martyr who himself was martyred for his faith was a bishop who ministered in the early second century. He freely wrote about such findings. In his *Second Apology* addressed to the Christians and delivered to the senate of Rome, he spoke of Neptune and Pluto, explaining that 'it was the angels and *those demons* who had been begotten by them that did these things to men, and women, and cities ...etc'.[14]

Further tales of the son of Prometheus, Deucalion, historic wars of giants – the Titans fought against Saturn. The fabled Cyclops, Hercules and Achilles. All these gods and demi-gods came about by way of the sexual union of fallen celestial beings with humankind. Apparently both sexes of angelic being lusted after 'strange flesh' and both sexes produced offspring. The war against heaven is recorded by Homer, Plato, Lucan and Seneca. Greek gods, Roman gods, Egyptian gods, Assyrian and Mesopotamian gods all perished in the mighty waters of the flood. Ezekiel 31 seems to give a detailed account of the judgment upon these legions of Satan.

When we begin to realise what really happened some 5,500-6,000 years ago, it makes perfect sense that coming down through the ages, various levels and the pace of knowledge was slowed down until the last 100 years or so. Only then was there a gearing up of great knowledge. I wonder why that would be?

---

14. Justin Martyr's Second Apology, chapter 5; see www.newadvent.org Justin Martyr's 'second apology' (accessed 4.7.20).

7. The Nephilim After the Flood

It would be completely remiss of me not to try to deal with the obvious question that arises from the previous chapter. Did all the Nephilim alive at the time of the flood perish in the flood, or did some miraculously survive? How come there were Nephilim (giants) after the flood? It is clear from biblical records quoted down through the generations that only eight people survived the flood. Noah, his wife, his three sons, Shem, Ham and Japheth and their wives. No one, human being or beast, bird or crawling thing survived.

What is also clear is that there were many Nephilim later on in the generations to come. How is that even possible? The answer could be one of two scenarios.

1. A repeat of the sins of 'the sons of God' (angels) occurred post-flood.
2. The genes of the Nephilim were carried in the bloodline of one of Noah's family.

I certainly hold to the second viewpoint. The first I don't see as possible, as from the flood onwards the angels 'who did not keep their proper domain [position]' were chained in the grave until the end of the age (Jude 6-7).

As for any other unfallen angel repeating the same sinful actions, the dreadful lessons were evident to see. The Most High God brought their mission to an abrupt and spectacular end. The likelihood is that one of the eight people was carrying the genes in their blood. But who?

Once Noah and his family had disembarked, life had to experience something of a 'reboot' – a restart. God said 'be fruitful and multiply' (Genesis 9:1,7). A rainbow was given as a supernatural sign that when it began to rain again, not to worry or be afraid; God was not going to flood the earth again – great comfort after the experience they just had.

The family of Noah began to rebuild their lives and start afresh, probably using much of the wood and materials from the ark in their construction of new homes. We go on to hear Noah 'planted a vineyard' (verse 20) and his son Shem had a son two years after the flood – Arphaxhad (Genesis 11:10-11).

It turns out to be Ham's wife who seems to be the carrier of the Nephilistic gene. Ham had a son with his wife. His name was Canaan. Here was the first subtle inference that something was, shall we say, different. Let's fast forward for a moment.

Noah planted this vineyard and one night thought he'd give his produce a really good testing. After a bout of quaffing his best vintage, Noah got drunk, for some reason was naked, and fell asleep. Ham found his father, and instead of discreetly covering him up, he seemed to go to his brothers Shem and Japheth and made fun of his father. His brothers were not amused and went to their father, entering his presence discreetly and carefully, not setting eyes on his nakedness and shame. They covered him with a sheepskin or the like. In the morning Noah was completely aware of what had happened. He cursed Ham's son Canaan in response to his embarrassment and shame. We do not know why this was. It's speculation, but maybe Noah knew there was something different about Canaan? Something amiss? Anyhow, he curses him. Here is the passage of Scripture:

> So Noah awoke from his wine, and knew what his younger son had done to him. Then he said: 'Cursed be Canaan;
> A servant of servants
> He shall be to his brethren.'
> And he said:

'Blessed be the Lord,
The God of Shem,
And may Canaan be his servant.
May God enlarge Japheth,
And may he dwell in the tents of Shem;
And may Canaan be his servant.
(Genesis 9:24-27)

In a moment Canaan had been sentenced to a life of subservience to his brothers. This would begin to play out over the next few centuries. This is where it gets really interesting. Let's look at the genealogies of Noah's sons.

> Now this *is* the genealogy of the sons of Noah: Shem, *Ham*, and Japheth. And sons were born to them after the flood.
>
> The sons of Japheth were Gomer, Magog, Madai, Javan, Tubal, Meshech, and Tiras. The sons of Gomer were Ashkenaz, Riphath, and Togarmah. The sons of Javan were Elishah, Tarshish, Kittim, and Dodanim. From these the coastland *peoples* of the Gentiles were separated into their lands, everyone according to his language, according to their families, into their nations. The sons of Ham were *Cush*, Mizraim, Put, and *Canaan*. The sons of *Cush* were Seba, Havilah, Sabtah, Raamah, and Sabtechah; and the sons of Raamah were Sheba and Dedan.
>
> *Cush* begot *Nimrod*; he began to be a mighty one on the earth. He was a mighty hunter before the LORD; therefore it is said, 'Like *Nimrod* the mighty hunter before the LORD.' And the beginning of his kingdom was Babel, Erech, Accad, and Calneh, in the land of Shinar.
>
> ...
>
> and Resen between Nineveh and Calah (that is the principal city).

> Mizraim begot Ludim, Anamim, Lehabim, Naphtuhim, Pathrusim, and Casluhim (from whom came the Philistines and Caphtorim).
>
> *Canaan* begot *Sidon* his firstborn, and *Heth*; the *Jebusite*, the *Amorite*, and the *Girgashite*; the *Hivite*, the *Arkite*, and the *Sinite*; the *Arvadite*, the *Zemarite*, and the Hamathite. Afterward the families of the Canaanites were dispersed. And the border of the Canaanites was from Sidon as you go toward Gerar, as far as Gaza; then as you go toward Sodom, Gomorrah, Admah, and Zeboiim, as far as Lasha. These were the sons of *Ham*, according to their families, according to their languages, in their lands and in their nations.
>
> (Genesis 10:1-10,12-20)

I've purposely put in italics the main players here that are extremely worthy of note. Following Ham's line and Canaan and Cush's line in particular, the Bible begins to add information to the genealogy. This is only ever done when the writer had something significant to show us. Cush and Canaan were brothers. The likelihood is that they were also carriers of the Nephilim gene. Cush has a son called Nimrod – which literally means 'to rebel'. Nimrod is an infamous character. A 'mighty hunter before the LORD'. The word for 'mighty' here is the same as for the Nephilim or giant.[15] This is more than likely the very first post-flood Nephilim. He becomes a builder of cities, he's a murderer and idolator, and becomes king of Babylon. He's known in historical records as the father of sorcery, of divination and human sacrifice. He went onto build the Tower of Babel in an attempt to rebel against God.[16] [17]All his days he pitches war against the Almighty.

---

15. Also see 'Who Were the Nephilim in the Bible?', www.Christianity.com (accessed 27.7.20).
16. See also Josephus, Flavius Antiquities of the Jews, Chapter 4 www.gutenberg.org (accessed 27.7.20)
17. Nimrod – Who was he? Was he godly or evil? www.christiananswers.net (accessed 27.07.20).

Canaan begets Sidon, *who becomes the father of all the Canaanites.* These Canaanite tribes end up covering the land that was to be promised to Noah's descendant, Abraham. By that time the Nephilim were ruling in the so-called Promised Land. These Nephilim went on to be called Rephaim (giants).[18]

Another character here worthy of note is Heth. He crops up in the genealogy of Canaan. He is the father of Arba (Joshua 14:13-15) who built Kirjath-arba, otherwise known as Hebron, one of the oldest cities in the known world. Arba, like his father Heth, was a Nephilim king. He gave birth to the sons of Arba, also called the Anakim.

According to the commandment of the Lord to Joshua, he gave to Caleb, the son of Jephunneh, a portion among the people of Judah, Kiriath-arba, that is, Hebron (Arba was the father of Anak). The Bible is totally clear on these enclaves of the Nephilim. They were sentenced to destruction by God, and were eventually executed via Joshua once he had crossed over the Jordan river into the Promised Land (Joshua 11:21).

Moses had previously had his battles with the Rephaim and Nephilim along the way. They destroyed completely the Nephilim kings of Sihon of the Amorites, a tribe of Nephilim. Perhaps the most feared was Og of Bashan, a Nephilim[19] and particularly powerful, with sixty stonewall cities in Argob (Deuteronomy 3:1-6).

Moses set the tone for Joshua to go on ahead and defeat the Nephilim wherever they found them. The truth, however, is the children of Israel were so terrified when their spies first saw the Anakim that their hearts melted (Joshua 14:8). Despite Caleb's brave statement that they should 'go up at once and take possession, for we are well able to overcome it' – with God they were well able to

18. See 'A Nation of Giants', www.hebrewuniversity.com; Rephaim, 'Gigantic races of Canaanites', www.biblehub.com (accessed 22.06.20).

19. See www.gotquestions.org Og's bed reportedly 13.5 ft long & 6 ft wide.

overcome them – the ten spies convinced the people that this was a suicidal mission.

Terrified, the children of Israel were not allowed to enter the land until another forty years had passed by and a new generation led by Joshua and Caleb took the Canaanite lands and vanquished the Nephilim. Only a small number were left after Joshua's military campaigns. On several occasions the Lord God even took matters into His own hands to destroy this semi-human race (Joshua 10:11-13).

The last of the giants are found in David's era. The mighty men were back. David himself whilst still a shepherd boy slew Goliath with his sling. Goliath was one of the last of the Nephilim (1 Samuel 17:4-7).

Here is Goliath. A Philistine Giant of about 9-10ft tall. A descendant of the Nephilim. The fact that David overcame him with his little sling is nothing short of a miracle. David took up five smooth stones but fired only one. It's often been said Goliath had several kinsmen. One of his brothers (2 Samuel 21:18-22). Maybe he was prepared for them too. Now we can at least begin to understand why God instructed His servants to literally wipe out and eradicate all communities whose bloodlines had been infiltrated by that of the Nephilim. It seems extraordinarily cruel, but it was the only way to eliminate the 'new species' and stop it arising again in the bloodline, just like we saw through Ham and his descendants.

> Yet again there was war at Gath, where there was a man of great stature, who had six fingers on each hand and six toes on each foot, twenty-four in number; and he also was born to the giant. So when he defied Israel, Jonathan the son of Shimea, David's brother, killed him. These four were born to the giant in Gath, and fell by the hand of David and by the hand of his servants.
> (2 Samuel 21:20-22)

These were probably the last of the bloodline of the Nephilim as we do not hear about them again. Their genetic bloodline was erased and Satan could no longer rely on his most diabolical of schemes. That would not, of course, stop him plotting and scheming his way to try to stop the coming of 'the promised one', the Messiah, who would crush the serpent's head and begin to put things back in order as regards God's plan for humankind, that of redemption – the code running down through the ages; God's plan to redeem His fallen creation back to Himself: 'through one man sin entered the world, and death through sin' (Romans 5:12). Therefore only one man could put it right. Not a 'son of God' but *the* Son of God; the Lord Jesus Christ; the Angel of the Lord, the Almighty One come to this world as a human being, that we as human beings might be able to enter into His world one day at the end of the war between heaven and hell.

8. Who's in Charge?

Whilst many of us believe in an ultimate supreme being, a 'higher power', God, a form of intelligence much higher than us, the Bible tells us that actually, the world is under the power and influence of Lucifer, the fallen angel also referred to as Satan, the devil, the Great Dragon, and serpent. John, one of the twelve disciples, writing in his third letter states clearly: 'We know that we [believers] are of God, and the whole world lies under the sway of the wicked one' (1 John 5:19). The NIV translation says, 'the whole world is under the control of the evil one.'

It is obvious from these words alone that there is a 'sub plot' at work in the world. Not all is as it seems. The apostle Paul says: 'in which you once walked according to the course of this world, according to the prince of the power of the air, the spirit who now works in the sons of disobedience' (Ephesians 2:2). Paul makes it very clear that someone other than humankind is in charge of the very atmosphere. Taken together with John's writings about the authority and control of 'the evil one', we can see that a power is operating which is incredibly influential, controlling and is working within people's lives all over the world.

Incredibly, this power can operate freely, and largely without being realised or recognised with almost perfect camouflage, as most people don't even believe 'the evil one' – 'the prince of the power of the air' – even exists! No wonder he's able to assume virtually full control of the world in which we live.

What is not realised is that there is a hierarchical world of the fallen powers, as referenced in Ephesians 6:12: 'For we do not wrestle against flesh and blood, but against principalities, against powers, against the rulers of the darkness of this age, against spiritual hosts of wickedness in the heavenly places.'

Here we have an incredible insight into the 'underworld' of Satan and his cohorts. A hierarchy of powers, with a rank and file of generals, captains, lieutenants and so on whose aim is to mastermind the subservience of the whole human race in order to get them all to 'worship him' like he initially wanted when he rebelled in heaven.

This leads me into seeking the 'exposure' of the enemy of our souls, his activities, his strategies and his ultimate aims. To turn all the world to him, to worship him, directly or indirectly, he's not bothered which, and to turn the tables on the God of creation, Jehovah, the Lord of all. The truth is, Jehovah's signature is on the whole of creation, it's in nature, within genetics, DNA, foliage and fauna and much, much more. Satan's signature is everywhere too. He actually copies God in many ways, and although incredibly powerful when compared to humankind – he even had power and authority over angelic beings – his power is hugely inferior compared to that of Almighty God, Jehovah. For instance, he cannot create life; he cannot read the mind or the heart; he does not know the future, nor does he completely understand the past. He is completely and totally deluded – self-deluded, actually.

Maybe you've come across this before, as I have. A person is caught lying, in deceit, maybe over a moral situation. They're found out. Exposed. Maybe the situation is so serious they lose their job, their marriage, status and respect. Then, whilst we try to maintain some kind of relationship with them, to maybe help them be healed, restored and to ultimately recover from the consequences of their dishonesty, they suddenly go into a kind of self-righteous, self-deceptive mode, leading to more lies, more deceit and perhaps even vindictive behaviour. Complete self-delusion is the inevitable outcome. This is so for Satan, who rebelled against his Creator. His end and his rebelliousness are recorded in the last book of the Bible, the book of Revelation.

> Then the beast was captured, and with him the false prophet who worked signs in his presence, by which he deceived those who received the mark of the beast and those who worshiped his image. These two were cast alive into the lake of fire burning with brimstone. And the rest were killed with the sword which proceeded from the mouth of Him who sat on the horse. And all the birds were filled with their flesh.
> (Revelation 19:20-21)

And again:

> Then I saw an angel coming down from heaven, having the key to the bottomless pit and a great chain in his hand. He laid hold of the dragon, that serpent of old, who is the Devil and Satan, and bound him for a thousand years; and he cast him into the bottomless pit, and shut him up, and set a seal on him, so that he should deceive the nations no more till the thousand years were finished. But after these things he must be released for a little while.
> (Revelation 20:1-3)

> The devil who deceived them, was cast into the lake of fire and brimstone where the beast and the false prophet are. And they will be tormented day and night forever and ever.
> (Revelation 20:10)

There is no doubting these verses, and for sure, even though Satan can read, he is wholly and totally self-deluded. He believes not only that he has a chance of winning this incredible battle, he actually believes he will win! To that end, the self-delusion continues, and he carries on with his evil strategies and schemes.

Satan's strategies: his goal and his aim

We have already established that Satan's aim is to get all humankind to worship him. Now let's take a look at the strategies he is using. He will stop at nothing in order to advance the cause of his own self-deluded worship. It's interesting to see how he uses certain methods to capture and enslave people spiritually. We will look at this in more detail in the next chapter.

9. Money, Power and Sex

Whilst what he uses may surprise you, we need to realise what enslaves and ensnares one person doesn't necessarily work with another. But Satan knows how to bait the hook; the outcome is nearly always slavery of one form or another through his deception. 'There'll always be fresh cheese in the mouse trap.' Here's a few of his strategies:

1. He uses money

To create greed, power, abuse, crime, violence, destruction.

> For the love of money is a root of all kinds of evil …
> (1 Timothy 6:10)

Note: 'Money' is not the root of all evil; *the love* of money is the root of all evil. There is absolutely nothing wrong with money in itself. It is vital to existence itself that we earn it, save it, invest it, donate it, give it and spend it too. But the 'love' of money results in greed, jealousy, envy, deceit, falsehood, crime and violence. The daily newspapers are always full of an almost endless variety of crimes committed to obtain more money.

People love money, and there is virtually nothing they will not do for it. People beg for it, sell their bodies for it, kill for it, lie for it, steal for it and all sorts of misery comes from it. Behind it is none other than 'the god of this world' (2 Corinthians 4:4, NRSV). Despite all this, obviously money can be used for good and we'd be in trouble without it. Jesus' attitude to it was just – well – incredibly healthy. He taught us about getting it, saving it, investing it, spending it and giving it. The problem comes when it gets into the wrong hands. That's when big trouble arrives.

Unfortunately, through the love of money, it has ended up mostly in hands that are corrupt, deceitful and avaricious. At the time of writing, 1 per cent of the population own 45 per cent of the world's wealth.[20] That's a bleak fact and it's probably going to get to the point where the number worsens. Satan uses the 'love' of money for so many negative things. That's manifestly obvious. His aim in doing so is misery, and spiritual enslaving of countless souls. That's why it comes in at No. 1 for me. I'm a Christian, and I have to confess, I do like money. I love spending it, who doesn't? But I really enjoy giving it away. There is a special 'release of joy and blessing' when you give money away. It's almost like you break any hold it has on you or over you. Consider Jesus words:

> It is more blessed to give than it is to receive.
> (Acts 20:35)

And from the book of Proverbs:

> There is one who scatters, yet increases more;
> And there is one who withholds more than is right,
> But it leads to poverty.
> The generous soul will be made rich,
> And he who waters will also be watered Himself.
> (Proverbs 11:24-25)

What we can see from these wise words is how 'giving' and 'releasing' do not lead into poverty as one might think.

It is my belief that generally speaking, those who are most wealthy tend to be those who are the most 'poor' in their souls. Many people have so much money they go off the rails. It literally ruins some

---

20. www.credit-suisse.com (accessed 27.07.20).

people. This is why some of the richest people in the world need to find a worthy cause to champion, a project that is humanitarian, as it literally brings a kind of 'release' – a blessing which is unique and very refreshing to the soul.

Steve Jobs, whilst terminally ill, was reported to have said: 'Being the richest man in the cemetery doesn't matter to me.'[21]

Some have died in anguish and loneliness, fear and depression, not being able to trust anyone, least of all their own relatives. One of the most common experiences I've seen over three decades of being a pastor, after a family member dies, is unknown, unheard of and unseen family members turning up out of the blue. That's so true, honestly, but, I'm afraid, also tragically sad. As someone once said, 'Where there's a will – there's a relative!'[22]

2. He uses power

Power can mean many things to so many people. It can be 'might or strength', as in a physical or military sense. It could also mean influence, even wealth. A king or queen, for instance, can be 'in power' for a season; another meaning could be authority, as in the power to permit, approve, decide or appoint something or someone. In all its facets, power is something the collective 'we' have strived for, for a long, long time. Wars are caused by the quest for more power. Blatant attempts to take over other countries by Adolf Hitler were ultimately the cause of the Second World War. Stalin, Pol Pot, Saddam Hussein and many more showed an insatiable desire for power, and even more power. We see it in politics too. It's amazing what lengths people will go to to get power. Treachery, betrayal, jealousy, envy have their roots in the love or need for power. As we have already seen, Lucifer fell from heaven due to his quest for more power. He became '*diabolos*' – the devil – because of such. So, power is something the devil uses

21. www.businessinsider.com 29 September 2015 (accessed 27.07.20).
22. Ricky Gervais. See www.brainyquote.com (accessed 27.07.20).

today in many corrupt and malicious ways, bringing death, disease, famine, starvation, deceitfulness and misery to countless thousands of people worldwide.

Unfortunately, God's ultimate crown in creation (humankind) has also embraced this love for 'power' through which wickedness and evil often parade. Power in all its forms has a challenge all of its own, and if not handled correctly, leads to many examples of abuse. Satan, the devil, is a master at using 'power' and 'might' to obtain his goals, and it seems he will stop at nothing to acquire more of it in the world in which we live.

Amazingly, the Bible tells us that Satan used the attractiveness of power to try to deceive Jesus Christ while He was in the wilderness, fasting for forty days and nights. This moment was immediately just before his three and a half years of public miraculous ministry began – Jesus went on to change water into wine, stilled the storm, healed the blind, the lame, the deaf and the dumb, fed thousands of people with a few loaves and fishes, and raised Lazarus from the dead.

We read that just after Jesus was baptised that he went into the wilderness. Whilst there can be no doubt that this strategy of fasting for well over a month was very much a part of his preparation going into the next crucial phase of his life, it also seemed to present a good opportunity for Satan to bring his deceptive powers to the fore.

We read in the Gospels of three specific temptations (though of course there may have been many more). The ones that are mentioned are very interesting to say the least.

> 'If You are the Son of God, command that these stones become bread.'
> But He answered and said, 'It is written, "Man shall not live by bread alone, but by every word that proceeds from the mouth of God."'
> (Matthew 4:3-4)

The temptation was a direct attempt to undermine Jesus' power and impose that of Satan's over Christ.

> Then the devil took Him up into the holy city, set Him on the pinnacle of the temple, and said to Him, 'If You are the Son of God, throw Yourself down. For it is written: "He shall give His angels charge over you," and, "In their hands they shall bear you up, Lest you dash your foot against a stone."'
> (Matthew 4:4-6)

Jesus reaction is resolute: 'It is written again, "You shall not tempt the LORD your God"' (Matthew 4:7).

> Again, the devil took Him up on an exceedingly high mountain, and showed Him all the kingdoms of the world and their glory. And he said to Him, 'All these things I will give You if You will fall down and worship me.' Then Jesus said to him, 'Away with you, Satan! For it is written, "You shall worship the Lord your God, and Him only you shall serve."' Then the devil left Him, and behold, angels came and ministered to Him.
> (Matthew 4:8-11)

All the temptations are to do with 'power' and the third one is incredibly interesting in that Satan's quest continues to get all of creation, including the angels of heaven, all the celestial creation (heavenly beings of which there are at least several kinds) and all of humankind to worship him. Now he tries it on with God's own Son, Jesus. For him, *it's all about power and authority.*

Luke in his Gospel gives us deeper insight into the situation:

> Then the devil, taking Him up on a high mountain, showed Him all the kingdoms of the world in a moment of time. And

> the devil said to Him, 'All this authority I will give You, and their glory; for this has been delivered to me, and I give it to whomever I wish. Therefore, if You will worship before me, all will be Yours.'
> (Luke 4:5-7)

It is amazing how the devil claims that he has been given authority over all the earth – and that he can give it to whomever he wishes! How utterly fascinating! Maybe when we look at how powerful human beings on the earth can be, we would do well to realise this; the source may not be recognisable to most people.

Already we have established that the Bible actually teaches that the whole world is under Satan's control, but ultimately, we know that this control is restricted to time and limited by a higher power, that of Christ Himself.

Jesus came to them (His disciples) and said:

> All authority has been given to Me in heaven and on earth. Go therefore and make disciples of all the nations, baptizing them in the name of the Father and of the Son and of the Holy Spirit … and lo, I am with you always, even to the end of the age.
> (Matthew 28:18-20)

So, we see two claims: one of the devil, whose claim to being in authority appears to be backed up in scripture as he is 'the god of this world' (2 Corinthians 4:4, NRSV) at the moment. All the world lies in his control, remember (1 John 5:19).

The other claim is Jesus': 'All authority has been given to Me in heaven *and on earth*' (my italics). Someone here appears to be wrong, but in actual fact, they are both correct. Later in the book, you will see these two claims reconciled.

3. He uses sex

Here is another form of power. Since the beginning, the fall, sex became corrupted and controlled by Satan. Love turned so easily to lust. It has remained a source of great joy, beauty, ecstasy and bliss – whilst at the same time the source of great pain, destruction, addiction, jealousy, envy, slavery and distortion. How is that even possible? But we all know it is. Ask any husband/wife/partner who has been cheated on. They will tell you of the pain of rejection, the sorrow of lost love.

It seems today we are close to overdosing on an epidemic of 'sexualisation' in our world. It is literally everywhere you look (and even where you don't!). It sells everything from cars to chocolate, perfume to holidays, clothes to food items. It is without doubt one of the biggest drivers in society. With the advancement of technology, pornography is just a click away. There seems to be an endless stream of sites that will hook you up with a 'sex partner'. Porn is now by far the most active online industry. The numbers are staggering! There are even robots being created that are designed to be able to have sexual intercourse with men or women.

It seems that there is a drive to be able to have a 'good sex life' without any true intimacy or an emotional 'tag' being placed upon us. This in turn is leading us, as human beings, to becoming almost incapable of healthy, intimate, close relationships, which require trust, core values, honesty, love, integrity, fidelity, loyalty to make them work properly.

We are moving towards a non-relational, mechanical, non-emotional, soulless world – i.e. sex without love. Yet, without love, sex becomes an act that is meaningless, self-gratifying, gratuitous, vacuous. Everything it was designed not to be. We were designed, created, to love and to be loved, and despite our imperfections since the fall, still many couples avow to keep believing in a covenant relationship called 'marriage'. Even when this does go awry, there remains the desire to try again, to have that secure, stable relationship that gives us far more than physical sexual satisfaction and pleasure.

Despite God creating sex as a most wonderful thing between a man and a woman, this is now being corrupted, leading to a downward spiral. Sex used to be so 'wow' amazing! But as Isaac Thomas said, 'Since sex got easier to get, love got harder to find.'[23]

There can be no doubt who is controlling the strings today as regards sexual power. The 'prince of the power of the air' (Ephesians 2:2) is well at work over the airwaves, making it a powerful domain of his. Just like the fruit of the tree of the knowledge of good and evil in Eden's garden, sex looks great and pleasurable to the eyes and sweet to the taste, but the consequences of partaking of it outside the boundaries of its parameter can be catastrophic. Nevertheless, this is also a stronghold that can be conquered through faith in Jesus Christ. He can restore us and our relationships to be lived out as God intended, in order to bring about the maximum pleasure and fulfilment within a healthy, fulfilling, emotionally stable environment.

Other strategies

The Bible often talks about 'strongholds' both in the Old Testament and in the New.[24] In the New Testament, these 'strongholds' are often very spiritual, psychological, mental and emotional. For example, today, alcohol, drugs, pornography, sexual addictions are strategies used to imprison people and keep them in a state of captivity, often leading to poor mental health, low self-esteem and, in many cases, severe depression and even suicidal thoughts. The 'self-destructive' capacity of such conditions is incredibly powerful and sadly well-documented.

23. Isaac Thomas, 23 November 2017, www.medium.com (accessed 27.07.20).
24. See 1 Samuel 5:7; 2 Corinthians 10:4.

We were not created to be subjected to any power other than our Creator's. Once we start to establish a meaningful, truthful relationship with our Creator, we start to find peace, satisfaction and most importantly, our true purpose, spiritually, emotionally and mentally.

If we start to live outside the parameters of our 'intended' purpose, tension, anxiety and stress start to become the norm.

We are certainly designed to withstand a great deal of pressure and strain, but there are types of pressure that are not good for us (think boundaries and borders spoken of in Chapter Two).

The minute we start to engage personally with our Creator is the minute things start to progress. It's no coincidence that to get the best results out of any product you buy, the best thing to do is to 'follow the maker's instructions'. I'll return to this thought a little later in the book. Until then, let's dig a little deeper into the code: Code Red.

10. Red is for Blood

We have seen already from the 'book of beginnings' – Genesis – that God instituted a strategy that was to enable the 'sin condition' to be dealt with. The first animal to be killed was by God Himself. He clothes the naked couple who had previously clothed themselves with aprons/tunics of fig leaves, which represents our own efforts to cover our shame and nakedness. This is typical of what we do today with all sorts of soulless religion, self-help and our own futile attempts to find inner peace, happiness and soul satisfaction. The trouble is, none of those things work properly, and fall short of acceptability in God's sight. Our nakedness and shame must be covered with something entirely different. Something that resembles 'life'. Created life; not propagated life as in vegetation (fig leaves) but created life i.e. animal skins.

The Bible clearly teaches that the blood of bulls and goats cannot atone for sin. This is made clear in the ninth chapter of the book of Hebrews in the New Testament.

> Not with the blood of goats and calves, but with His own blood He entered the Most Holy Place once for all, having obtained eternal redemption. For if the blood of bulls and goats and the ashes of a heifer, sprinkling the unclean, sanctifies for the purifying of the flesh, how much more shall the blood of Christ, who through the eternal Spirit offered Himself without spot to God, cleanse your conscience from dead works to serve the living God?
> (Hebrews 9:12-14)

As we have already seen, the first sacrifice for sin was an animal in Eden (Genesis 3:21). We don't know exactly what kind of animal was killed and used. It's likely it was a sheep, and lamb's skin was used, as it would fulfil the typological pattern of Abel bringing the sacrifice of a lamb (Genesis 4:4). Note: the lamb was now instituted in the mind of Adam, Eve and their sons as an acceptable sacrifice to God. However, Cain's offering was of the ground and therefore it was unacceptable to God (Genesis 4:3,5-7).

We see here clearly what is acceptable in God's sight. Here, clearly begins the code that is red. All the sacrifices from Eden until Solomon's Temple and even later on, in Herod's Temple, were continually pointing to one thing. The coming of Messiah, the Anointed One, Christ Jesus.

> The next day John saw Jesus coming toward him, and said, 'Behold! The Lamb of God who takes away the sin of the world! ... Behold the Lamb of God!'
> (John 1:29,36)

John the Baptist declares the redemptive plan of heaven in one simple but profound statement: 'Behold the Lamb of God!' This is 'the One' *all* sacrifices that had ever been made pointed to. Those sacrifices were only animals. This sacrifice would be human, it was voluntary and it was unique.

The concept of sacrifice, of course, was nothing new. All of the religions practised it. Some practised human sacrifice, even child sacrifice. The concept has been corrupted by evil, wicked people who instituted sacrifices to idols and even themselves, but nevertheless, the one, true sacrifice for all the sins of the world was none other than Jesus Christ, the Lamb of God. Here, in front of us is the direct link to that moment in Genesis in the Garden of Eden, when the sin of Adam and Eve was discovered. The death of that first animal pointed to the one death that would cover all our sin, forever.

Since the beginning of time, Code Red has been in operation right up until this present day. That is why there is now *no need* for any animal sacrifice to be made, because Jesus died upon the cross of Calvary. Once and for *all*!

> Who does not need daily, as those high priests, to offer up sacrifices, first for His own sins and then for the people's, for this He did once for all when He offered up Himself.
> (Hebrews 7:27)

> By that will we have been sanctified through the offering of the body of Jesus Christ once and for all.
> (Hebrews 10:10)

Here it is, clearly written and precise, the sacrifice of Christ has been made 'once and for all', for everyone.

At this point, I want to share a most fascinating story from the Scriptures, from the book of Joshua, to close our chapter. It's about a woman called Rahab, and she was a prostitute. She lived in a city called Jericho. The city was an impregnable fortified city. The army of Joshua was about to cross the Jordan river and conquer everything in sight and take possession of the land called Canaan. Most of the inhabitants were not worried in the slightest. The walls of Jericho were at least 5ft thick, possibly 7ft: there seem to have also been a secondary wall with similar thickness. These walls were about 20ft tall, possibly more. Within these walls, houses were built. Rahab's house was one such house (Joshua 2:15).

Joshua had sent two spies out to check out the city. The two spies came to Rahab's house. The king of Jericho heard the two men had entered the city and that they were at Rahab's house. The king sent men to her house and requested the spies be brought out. Rahab lied to protect the men, and hid them in her home. She told the king's men that they had gone out at night and if they pursued them, they would catch them. So the king's men did exactly that.

The spies were lowered down the wall, through a window. Before Rahab did this she said to the men that she knew that their God was the one true God, and pleaded with them to spare her and her family's lives. The men promise she will be saved only if she stays in the confines of the house. The condition of this 'pact' was that she should tie a scarlet thread outside her window. She did this, and the spies escaped.

This story is not about morality. *It's about faith.* When the walls of Jericho came falling down, there was a part that was left untouched, that of Rahab and her family (Joshua 2:18-19).

Once the walls had fallen down, Joshua told the two spies to go to Rahab's house and bring out the woman and her family. Her life was spared (Joshua 6:25). Her faith saved her and her family on that day, just like the blood on the doorposts in Egypt saved the Hebrews. Code Red had once again been in action. The red blood of the lamb painted on the lintels of the doors of the Hebrews has saved their firstborn being struck by the angel of death (Exodus 12:7; 12-13).

Can you see what is happening here? Code Red is in full swing! The scarlet thread, the blood on the doorposts? It all adds up to one marvellous fact: the blood of Jesus, the Lamb of God, distinguishes us from those destined for destruction and disaster. Only the fact that Jesus died upon the cross can defeat the curse; this is clearly what is being shown. This is the only way we overcome it! This is the way we triumph over evil, over darkness, and the 'god of this world' (2 Corinthians 4:4, NRSV).

One last thought on Rahab before we move on. Rahab pops up again in Jewish history as an example of faith and forgiveness. The next reference we should look at is just as incredible: 'Salmon begot Boaz by Rahab, Boaz begot Obed by Ruth, Obed begot Jesse, and Jesse begot David the king' (Matthew 1:5-6). How incredible that we find a Canaanite woman, a former prostitute, who is married to Salman and gives birth to Boaz, a rich man, who marries Ruth, the great-grandmother of King David! Who do you think eventually comes from David's lineage? None other than Jesus, the Lamb of God. And genetically, Code Red is generationally flowing down through the ages, and continues unto this present day.

Rahab also appears in the 'Gallery of Faith' in Hebrews as a hero of the faith, alongside Abraham, Moses, Gideon, David and Samuel (Hebrews 11:31). This is just amazing and shows the incredible power and grace of God's forgiveness and mercy and acceptance.

Code Red is about redemption and regeneration from Eden until this present day, with the cross being the centrepiece in the middle of the process. Still the cross stands in the centre of it all, BC/AD, Before Christ and after Christ.

11. What Language Has to Say

When you purchase a product, be it electrical or a functional appliance of some kind, you will receive amongst its voluminous packaging some form of instruction on how to set up the appliance, and how to use it. I love the saying: 'For the best results follow the maker's instructions'. It makes perfect sense, and can often save an enormous amount of time, unless you're like me and often think, 'It's OK, I've got this', only to find yourself backtracking and beginning to read the instructions once you're stuck in assembly mode!

Within each of God's creation, He has placed an 'in-built language'. It's called DNA. It is nothing short of miraculous when observed under the right conditions.

These next few chapters we are going to dive right into that phenomena. Not just DNA, but language itself. It may be of interest to you to know that our records of a proper spoken and written language only dates back to 3,000-3,500 BC i.e. it is only 5,000-6,000 years old at the most.[25] To me that is incredibly significant. 'Why?' you might ask. Well, we are constantly taught that humanity has been around for millions of years. At least hundreds of thousands of years. This means humankind only began to communicate properly, by language, 5-6,000 years ago. What on earth has humanity been doing for the millions of years before that? I cannot believe for a single moment that humankind developed that slowly and then all of a sudden, boom! Somebody invented, created, a language!

When you consider the rate of development down through the ages – Stone Age, Bronze Age, Iron Age, Medieval Age, Industrial Age, Modern Age, Postmodern Age – until now, covering several

---

25. See www.holidify.com; www.daytranslations.com (accessed 7.6.20). Many more sources online.

thousand years, the idea of humankind being stuck in a bubble of underdevelopment, inertia and frozen thinking is much harder to believe, to me, than the following thesis: that the Genesis record of the Bible is true historically and genealogically too. Genesis 10, as we've already seen, is, according to the Bible, the earliest, most credible, accurate, detailed record we possess today if we wish to trace back the birth of tongues, tribes and nations. The book of Genesis has an identifiable timeline (whether one agrees with it or not is another matter) of 5-6,000 years since the Tower of Babel. Here at the Tower of Babel, languages were given to humankind in order to divide and scatter the people and family groups among the earth at that time.

The Bible teaches that pre-Babel all the world spoke the same language (Genesis 11:1). That is, until they pushed too far and too hard to reach the heights of heaven (Genesis 11:8). This took place, according to the Genesis timetable, about 6,000 years ago (4,000 BC). The oldest languages known to us are ancient Egyptian, Sumerian, Chinese, Ancient Greek and those of the Asiatic tribes, Sanskrit and Tamil. Hebrew, of course, was an early language, but certainly younger than ancient Egyptian or that spoken by the Chaldeans in Ur of the Chaldees, Mesopotamia, the areas of Iran and Iraq, previously Persia and Medo-Persia.

It is, therefore, not beyond the bounds of possibility that the earliest language spoken from the ancient times previous to Babel was Tamil.

Ancient Arabic is, of course, related to Islam, though Islam came much later at about AD500. Ancient Hebrew came probably from a derivative of the Chaldean language, as we know Abraham, the father of all the Hebrews, came out of Mesopotamia. Hebrew has always been the mother tongue of Israel, Israel being synonymous with Jacob, the father of the twelve tribes of Israel. Ancient Greek much later was connected to Christianity, Sanskrit related to Hinduism, Korean and

Chinese language is connected to Buddhism, Taoism, whilst Tamil is not linked to a specific religion and is spoken by some 80-100 million people still to this day. India, Sri Lanka, Malaysia and Indonesia are a few countries that still speak Tamil. I've placed this possibility in this chapter simply as a way of saying, language in itself by way of its timeline in history certainly concurs with the Genesis record. Just as language within our speech and literature gives some voracity to the Genesis creation record, so do other forms of language. Such as DNA, music and even technology.

The study of language is incredibly revealing. Most of us do not stop to think where they came from or who invented them, let alone how old they may be.

Language is developing all the time. There are many new languages today that have surfaced over the past few years. New languages have sprung up in northern Australia, for example. A closer study had found this language came about through children at school mixing older languages with new dialects. Esperanto, of course, was a newly fabricated language meant to unite the whole of Europe. It was spoken by a number of European politicians. Billionaire George Soros is fluent in Esperanto. New languages were created for the TV series *Game of Thrones*. Valyrian and also Dothraki were made just for the series, but they are languages nonetheless. These are actual languages made up by David Peterson. They used ancient Egyptian language along with several Bantu tongues as well as more than a trace of Latin and Classical Arabic.

When we look back to the time of Genesis 10, we see the postdiluvian age, as it's called after the great global flood. Whilst Tamil or Sanskrit are the common choices amongst the leading linguists for being the oldest languages in the world, there is one that stands out when it comes to its witness of things biblical and recorded in the Genesis record.

Chinese has several variants, Mandarin and Cantonese bring two of the obvious ones. Ancient Chinese is one of those classical pictorial languages with individual characters being made up of small drawings integrated together to signify an idea, concept or word.

Mouth + man = Older Brother

Tolal + Waters = Flood

Examples are: combinations of these small drawings are used to invoke historical events then widely accepted to describe terms.

Dust + Breath + Alive = To Talk

So, for instance, the concepts of dust, breath and 'alive' amounts to 'talk':

To talk + Walking = To Create

> And the Lord God formed man *of* the dust of the ground, and breathed into his nostrils the breath of life; and man became a living being.
> (Genesis 2:7)

丿 + 土 + 儿 = 先

Alive Dust man First

The combination of 'man', 'dust' and 'living' = 'first'

This is no fluke, either, as the formula continues in even more obvious ways, e.g.: 'happiness' is a combination of the characters for 'God', 'one', 'man' and 'garden'. This is not coincidental. The word for 'cruel' or 'violent' is made up of the characters for 'mouth' and 'man' – put the character for 'mouth' on the top of the character for 'man', it becomes 'eldest son'. Add the character for 'cover' into the middle of the character for 'mouth' and the combination of the three characters means 'violent' or 'cruel' – straight from the first murder of a man according to Genesis.

口 + 儿 = 兄 兇

Mouth man Eldest son Cruel Violent

> Now Cain [eldest brother] talked [mouth] with Abel his brother; and it came to pass, when they were in the field, that Cain [eldest brother] rose up against Abel his brother and killed him.
>
> (Genesis 4:8)

Our final example is for me not only striking, it is emphatically clear. The word for a 'flood' is made up of characters for 'person', the number 'eight' and for 'boat'.

口 + 八 + 舟 = 船

Person Eight Boat Large Ship

There are many more examples I could give, if the reader wants to study this. The words for temptation are a picture of a tree, two people and a serpent. Other languages apart from Chinese which are pictorial also have similar connotations. Ancient Egyptian, with its hieroglyphs, and Mesopotamian have similar references to biblical events.

Personally, I don't think it's surprising that written into the meaning of language is some of the main historical events that affected us all. Creation, the fall of humanity, the worldwide flood, the Tower of Babel, and great earthquakes and disease, lunar and solar eclipses, together with any other unexplained astronomical activities, we would expect to be woven into historical language. Most ancient tribal groups have an ancient story of a great flood. It's only surprising if you never thought of it being actually true before.

On its own, the inclusion of biblical events that brought meaning and definition to ancient languages doesn't prove that much, so let's look at another language – the language of music.

12. The Language of Music

We now turn to another language. That of music.

In terms of the origin of music, Jubal 'was the father of all those who play the harp and flute' (Genesis 4:21). This is the first reference to music we have in any historical documents. Probably dating back to about 4,500BC. The next time we read about music in the Bible is when the Children of Israel crossed the Red Sea (Exodus 15:20). No doubt music became part of everyday life, especially celebrations, events and in the capture of special moments. It is evident from Scripture that music is part of heavenly and celestial activity, directed to worship God by angels and other celestial beings (Revelation 5:8-9; 15:3).

My main aim here is to show that music did not start on earth, it was already practised in heaven. Actually, there are three distinct things that started in heaven, not earth.

1. Fire (the first inference of fire is in Genesis when God clothed the fallen couple with animal skins to replace their fig leaves – the carcass was undoubtedly burnt as a sacrifice showing Cain and Abel the example of offering sacrifices for themselves). Fire is God's gift to humankind which is both life-giving, a giver of warmth, purifying in cooking and useful for light. (It can also be deadly if used wrongly.)
2. Language. As we've already seen in our previous chapter, language has been around since the beginning of creation. There are languages in heaven and on earth. These are distinct as described by Paul in the New Testament, when he refers to the 'tongues of men and of angels' (1 Corinthians 13:1).
3. Singing/music. We read on the morning of creation 'the morning stars sang together, And all the sons of God [angels] shouted for joy' (Job 38:7).

The context here shows that music and singing were already in existence before the earth's foundation was laid.

Ezekiel goes on to describe Lucifer as a being that had musical ability designed within his very being:

> You were in Eden, the garden of God;
> Every precious stone was your covering:
> The sardius, topaz, and diamond,
> Beryl, onyx, and jasper,
> Sapphire, turquoise, and emerald with gold.
> The workmanship of your timbrels and pipes
> Was prepared for you on the day you were created.
> (Ezekiel 28:13)

Many believe Lucifer was the main worship leader in heaven, until he fell when his desire to be worshipped – 'like the Most High' (Isaiah 14:14) – got the better of him and in his pride and jealousy he fell.

These three things (fire, music and language) emanated from heaven – not earth, according to the Scriptures – so are pretty much timeless.

The Hurrian Hymn No. 6

Getting back to music, the earliest historical fragment of music we have is a 4,000-year-old Sumerian clay tablet called the 'Hurrian Hymn No. 6'. It is a hymn of worship to the goddess Nikkal, which was found in the ancient city of Ugarit in northern Syria. It is an amazing piece of music, and you can even hear it being played if you google it. It is very melodic, despite its age, and has been reproduced on instruments commensurate with that age frame. What is amazing is when you see the written notes.[26]

26. https://.youtu.be/QpxN2VXPMLc (accessed 29.7.20).

What is also amazing, though, is how we lost that language of music, only for Johan Sebastian Bach to pick it back up (or something very similar) in the use of a similar musical language, using notes and scales used in Gregorian chants.[27]

Johan Sebastian Bach once said: 'I play the notes as they are written, but it is God who makes the music.'[28] How right he was. Unfortunately, as with all good gifts, they can be corrupted, abused and used for the wrong things. Bach was, of course, credited with many wonderful pieces of music including 'Jesu, Joy of Man's Desiring' (which happened to be my father's favourite piece of music), 'Air on the G String', 'St Matthew Passion', 'Toccata and Fugue in D Minor', to name just a few. He is considered by many to be the greatest composer of all time, though he wrote primarily for churches in his early days, but he ended up playing, composing and performing for royalty.[29] Many composers and musical geniuses followed in his footsteps. Bach, however, is probably the father of the written sheet music we have today.

My point in bringing music into this book is because it is essentially spiritual, inspirational, therefore moving, and frankly, after all I've put forth, an obvious 'gift from God' to us all.

As an avid sports fan of golf, football, rugby league, I've seen how music has played such an important role. I am, as many know, a lifelong Liverpool fan. When I was writing this book, I was enjoying possibly the greatest ever Liverpool team to emerge, which was something I never expected could happen again. When I was growing up as a kid on Merseyside, I supported my team when we had Tommy Smith, Joey Jones, John Toshack, Phil Neal, 'Crazy Horse' Emlyn Hughes

---

27. Written notation in music is attributed to monks of Arezzo in Italy. Especially to Guido of Arezzo in or around 1025. See www.wqxr.org (accessed 3.3.20).
28. www.sundaysocial.tv (accessed 3.3.20).
29. See 'Famous Sayings by Bach', www.goodreads.com; also, www.quotes.thefamouspeople.com (accessed 3.3.20).

as captain, Ray Clemence etc. but I found I was pinching myself at the records the team were breaking again. Coronavirus conspired to interfere, but we were sitting twenty-five points clear in March 2020.

The thing I love about my team that has always kept me a passionate fan, even in tough times, is our atmosphere, our anthem, our fans, our history, our singing. Our music! Other fans will have their moments too, I understand. But I've seen in sport the power and inspiration the singing fans can have on any team. Talk about the 'twelfth man' is well founded when it comes to the power of music. The power of anthems. Think of hymns like 'Guide Me, O Thou Great Jehovah' sung by a fully sold-out rugby match at Cardiff Arms Park. Especially against the English! It's almost like they are a try up when you hear that. 'Abide With Me' always brings tears to my eyes when I hear it sung at an FA Cup Final; I don't completely understand why. It has something to do with a huge number singing something godly, in my opinion. Something that's full of truth. There is no doubt in my mind that songs like this touch the spirits core. They carry a cry of redemption in them.

Guide Me, O Thou Great Jehovah[30]

Guide me, O Thou great Jehovah,
Pilgrim through this barren land;
I am weak, but Thou art mighty,
Hold me with Thy powerful hand.
Bread of heaven, Bread of heaven,
Feed me till I want no more;
Feed me till I want no more.

30. www.godtube.com (accessed 24.6.20).

Open now the crystal fountain,
Whence the healing stream doth flow;
Let the fire and cloudy pillar
Lead me all my journey through.
Strong Deliverer, strong Deliverer,
Be Thou still my Strength and Shield;
Be Thou still my Strength and Shield.

When I tread the verge of Jordan,
Bid my anxious fears subside;
Death of death and hell's Destruction,
Land me safe on Canaan's side.
Songs of praises, songs of praises,
I will ever give to Thee;
I will ever give to Thee.

William Williams (1717-91)
Music: '*Cwm Rhondda*', John Hughes (1873-1932)

It's extremely hard to sing these words without being moved. Lyrics that tell of our struggle in life, journeying through life's often barren land until we come to the verge of Jordan (death), and so on.

Even the theme of crossing over into the Promised Land is picked up, though biblically incorrect if you're being picky, as Canaan's side was full of problems. Giants, Jericho and enemies aplenty awaited – hardly an accurate picture of the divine, heavenly Promised Land called heaven where there will be no more tears, no more pain or suffering (Revelation 21:4). Nevertheless, such is the power of the truth of passing from death to life, from this life to the next; it resonates with both the singer and the listener to bring about a powerful emotion that quite frankly transcends sport and the triteness and frivolity of a simple game played between twenty-two men, two goals and a ball!

Abide with Me[31]

Abide with me; fast falls the eventide;
The darkness deepens; Lord, with me abide;
When other helpers fail and comforts flee,
Help of the helpless, oh, abide with me.

Swift to its close ebbs out life's little day;
Earth's joys grow dim, its glories pass away;
Change and decay in all around I see—
O Thou who changest not, abide with me.

I need Thy presence every passing hour;
What but Thy grace can foil the tempter's pow'r?
Who, like Thyself, my guide and stay can be?
Through cloud and sunshine, Lord abide with me.

I fear no foe, with Thee at hand to bless;
Ills have no weight, and tears no bitterness;
Where is death's sting? Where, grave, thy victory?
I triumph still, if Thou abide with me.

Hold Thou Thy cross before my closing eyes;
Shine through the gloom and point me to the skies;
Heaven's morning breaks, and earth's vain shadows flee;
In life, in death, o Lord, abide with me.

Henry Francis Lyte (1793-1847)
Music: 'Eventide', William Henry Monk (1823-89)

---

31. www.godtube.com (accessed 7.6.20).

This sacred hymn carries such a deep, comforting truth, it is used by many at funerals to bring comfort and solace to those who have been bereft of loved ones. It has a profound ability to draw out sorrow for us as we sing this last verse. So poignantly powerful it is, as to almost transport us from the temporal nature of this life to deeper thoughts of future eternal life and the huge gulf there is between the two.

The Code Red kicks in powerfully as we sing about such transformational truth. Many are moved when they sing this but don't know why. Others are unmoved because they don't know what it is they're truly singing about. But the music, the words, have a code running through it. It is definitely red!

One final hymn to leave with you is another of my all-time favourites, but seldom sung these days.

O Love That Wilt Not Let Me Go[32]

O love, that wilt not let me go,
I rest my weary soul in Thee;
I give thee back the life I owe,
That in Thine oceans depths its flow
May richer, fuller be.

O Light, that followest all my way,
I yield my flickering torch to Thee;
My heart restores its borrowed ray,
That in Thy sunshine's blaze its day
May brighter, fairer be.

O Joy, that seekest me through pain,
I cannot close my heart to Thee;

32. www.hymnal.net (accessed 28.7.20).

I trace the rainbow through the rain,
And feel the promise is not vain
That morn shall tearless be.

O cross that liftest up my head,
I dare not ask to fly from Thee;
I lay in dust's life's glory dead,
And from the ground there blossoms red
Life that shall endless be.

George Matheson (1842-1906)
Music: Albert L. Peace (1844-1912)

Matheson provided us with an account of the origins of this, one of the most beloved hymns of the late nineteenth century:

> My hymn was composed in the manse of Innellan on the evening of the 6th of June, 1882 … Something happened to me, which was known only to myself, and which caused me the most severe mental suffering. The hymn was the fruit of that suffering. It was the quickest bit of work I ever did in my life. I had the impression rather of having it dictated to me by some inward voice than of working it out myself.
>
> I am quite sure that the whole work was completed in five minutes, and equally sure it never received at my hands any retouching or correction. I have no natural gift of rhythm. All the other verses I have ever written are manufactured articles; this came like a dayspring from on high. I have never been able to gain once more the same fervour in verse.[33]

33. www.hymnal.net (accessed 28.7.20).

He wrote this hymn on the day of his sister's marriage. His fiancée had broken her engagement to him, telling him that she couldn't see herself going through life married to a blind man. Matheson never married, and it seems likely that his sister's wedding brought to memory the woman that he had loved and the wedding that he had never enjoyed.

At any rate, Matheson's 'severe mental suffering' inspired him to write this hymn. The hymn celebrates the constancy of God's love and concludes by celebrating 'Life that shall endless be'.

Another remarkable evidence of the language of music and song, echoing down through the ages, the Code Red of Christ's redemption from suffering and death. Surely you can now read the code for yourself? The code is clear – the code is red!

13. The Language of Science (DNA)

We have already covered a fair bit of ground in the area of creation and I've made my position clear. This part of the book, though controversial to some, will be a remarkable witness to others to the fact that we are living in bodies that are decaying and dying, and living in a world that seems destined to doom and destruction – however, there is still evidence of 'the code of redemption' virtually everywhere we look.

I'm going to give you several small chapters setting out these evidences. If you wish to research these in more depth there is a lot of new material available now more than ever from eminent scientists, geneticists, archaeologists, biologists, palaeontologists, chemists, who like me believe that a 'designer' is behind all life forms.[34] A Creator who is not cruel and has engineered a way of escaping judgement and the eventual 'wrath to come' (Matthew 3:7), via His plan of redemption for all who believe in Him.

If God really created the world and its inhabitants, plants, animals, fish, birds, and us too, then surely you'd find evidences of that within what He created. Well, surprise, surprise, that's exactly what He has done. Let's start with science. We know that the world orbits the sun. The moon orbits the earth. This gives us a precise and exact timeframe to enable us to continue to keep existing. The earth rotates at a tilted angle of 23.5 degrees. Over the course of a year, the earth's tilt does not vary at all. Without any orbiting going on, the earth would go crashing into the sun. If the earth was a fraction out, and say moved closer to the sun, it would have a devastating effect on our world. Likewise, if it moved away, that would be disastrous too:

34. See www.famousscientists.org; www.veritas.org; www.christianitytoday.org; www1.cbn.com; www.premierchristianity.com; www.icr.org; www.biologos.org (accessed 07.04.20).

my point being that everything is so finely balanced and fine-tuned. How amazing this is when you stop and think of the complexity of it all. Jeremiah the prophet said:

> Through the LORD's mercies we are not consumed …
> (Lamentations 3:22)

The reality of our very existence is by such fine margins that something has to be behind it all. Something or someone is controlling not just the natural cycle of life on earth, but the very universe itself. The world, however, has a unique environment, unlike any other planet. It has its own gravity and biodiversity, its own life cycles and its own uniquely special character. Everything is precisely geared towards enabling the population continuing to exist despite all the natural and unnatural disasters it has faced. It is like a huge solar-powered clock. If all that has happened has occurred by chance or by accident, I find that wholly incomprehensible and to put it frankly, unbelievable. It is no more possible that a computer being brought about by a series of accidents and so-called mutations. 'Impossible,' I hear you say. 'Exactly!' is my response.

The Code Red can be seen in the body too. DNA is a fairly recent discovery (1953) that has always existed. We just didn't know it for many thousands of years. Discoveries are simply an uncovering of what has always been there. The truth of DNA has been under our noses, so to speak, for so many years. Now, it tells us of an intricate language that could never have been brought about by a random act.

DNA is a language. It is information, a code that is present within every cell. We can get a good understanding of how it works by our use of the binary code. This code, which is much simpler than that of DNA, was invented by us. It did not happen by accident (I'm sure you get the point). In or around 1673 a man named Gottfried Leibniz invented the binary code. He published his invention in 1703. This language contains only two characters: 0 and 1. The then Duke of Brunswick issued a silver medal to Leibniz in which he inscribed, '*The model of creation discovered by G.W.L.*'

What is even more staggering is, there is now evidence to suggest that the ancient Egyptians used a similar code containing just two numbers. Isn't that mind-blowing? If indeed that is the case, I believe they had been influenced by other life forms from Genesis 6 and the visitation of the 'sons of God'.

In 1990, an international team of researchers began a project known as the Human Genome Project (HGP). This was to be an attempt to discover in depth, the sequencing and mapping of genes within human cells. The project took thirteen years and was completed in April 2003. It was a fascinating breakthrough moment. The HGP gave us the ability to read the genetic blueprint for constructing a human being. For the first time in history, we could read DNA just like you would read a language.

In March 2000, the HGP international consortium announced 3 billion letters (characters) that constitute the genetic codebook of humans have 'been deciphered and deposited into the Genbank'.[35] To explain this in an easier way, a comparison can be made with the binary code already mentioned. It is binary because only two letters, 0 and 1 (usually) are used. A decimal system uses ten numbers, of course. The binary code assigns a pattern of digits (also known as 'bits') to each character. A binary code number would look something like 011010010110. Amazingly, binary systems existed in the ancient world. As well as evidence for it in ancient Egypt, as I previously stated, China too had a similar code using the 'yin and yang' characters, giving rise to dualism. Yin is feminine, yang is masculine. Yin is dark, yang is light. It's a kind of negative-positive formula.

35. www.genome.gov (accessed 28.7.20).

In comparison of the binary code to DNA, the US government is able to identify everyone in the country by the arrangement of a nine-digit number for social security administration. At the same time, inside every human cell, there is a 3 billion-lettered DNA structure that belongs only to you. To be able to just begin to comprehend this fact, a live reading of that cell's code at a rate of three letters per second would take, wait for it, thirty-one years, even if reading continuously day and night without a break. Staggering, I think you'll agree. What is also amazing is 99.9 per cent of our DNA is similar to everyone else's DNA. What makes you unique is the sequencing of that DNA.[36] Simply put, DNA is a language all on its own, but it is built upon sequencing.

DNA is made up of four chemicals. These are thymine, guanine, adenine and cytosine. T, G, A and C. It is, furthermore, a two-stranded molecule that has a double helix shape. So, instead of being binary, e.g. '01100101101' it would read 'CTTGAGACTA' or similar. Interestingly, Perry Marshall, an information specialist, points out: 'There has never existed a computer programme that wasn't designed ... [whether it is] a code, or a program, or a message given through a language, there is always an intelligent mind behind it.'[37] Dr Antony Flew, once an atheist, questioned this in his own thinking too. Dr Flew was a leading activist in atheism, involved in many debates. It was discoveries like I've mentioned that, after thirty years, brought him to the conclusion that 'super-intelligence is the only good explanation for the origin of life and the complexity of nature'. The discoveries of DNA were prominent in his thinking, and led to him becoming a firm believer in a Creator. He also asked, 'who wrote this script? Who placed this working code inside the cell?'[38]

36. 'Is God Real?', www.everystudent.com (accessed 6.3.20).
37. Francis S. Collins, *The Language of God* (New York: Free Press, 2006).
38. 'Is God Real?', www.everystudent.com (accessed 28.7.20).

In Psalm 139:14-15 we read:

> I will praise You, for I am fearfully and wonderfully made;
> Marvelous are Your works,
> And that my soul knows very well.
> My frame was not hidden from You,
> When I was made in secret,
> And skillfully wrought in the lowest parts of the earth.

So, we can see these eminent professional experts in their field, restating and reasserting what is said in Scripture, whether they were aware of it at the time or not.

On 26 June 2000, President Bill Clinton congratulated those who had completed the HGP. He said, 'Today we are learning the language in which God created life. We are gaining ever more awe for the complexity, the beauty, the wonder of God's most divine and sacred gift.'[39] Dr Francis Collins, director of the Human Genome Project, followed Clinton to the podium, stating 'it is humbling for me and awe inspiring to realize that we have caught the first glimpse of our own instruction book, previously known only to God'.[40]

So, I think, in bringing this chapter to a conclusion, there is overwhelming evidence to support the belief that there is a much higher power or agency at work in creation, rather than a 'random' and 'ad-hoc' series of accidental events that happened to come together by chance and coincidence. The evidence is out there, as long as people are willing to challenge themselves.

39. 'Is God Real?', www.everystudent.com (accessed 28.7.20).
40. 'Is God Real?', www.everystudent.com (accessed 28.7.20).

14. Laminins Lighting the Way?

Moving on from the language of DNA, we have another great example of creation deep within our molecular structure, a strong indicator as to who our Creator actually is. Before we dive right into this matter, let's consider the claim of the disciple of Christ. That of John in the opening of his Gospel.

> In the beginning was the Word, and the Word was with God, and the Word was God. He was in the beginning with God. All things were made through Him, and without Him nothing was made that was made.
> (John 1:1-3)

This is quite some claim from John. He refers to 'The Word' (I've capitalised the definite article here according to the original translation) as being 'with God' and then 'The Word was God'. He then goes on to claim that 'He [The Word] made *all* things'! This is a hugely important verse in the Bible for every Christian, as our faith and trust is placed upon this sweeping claim. John goes on to be much more specific as to who he is talking about.

> And the Word became flesh and dwelt among us, and we beheld His glory, the glory as of the only begotten of the Father, full of grace and truth.
> (John 1:14)

So we see plainly the identity of 'The Word' who John is writing about. He is the Creator. It is God who has come down in human form at the incarnation. John is saying that He, Jesus, is not only God, He is the Creator too. The same one who was there in His pre-incarnated form at the beginning of time. John starts his Gospel at the beginning of creation. There isn't even a salutary greeting! It's just 'In the beginning was the Word'. It is just like the first verse of the Bible in Genesis, which starts 'In the beginning God'. In other words, there can be no doubt at all about the voracity and authority with which John is declaring Jesus as the supreme Creator and, of course, one with The Father.

And so we come to 'laminins'. These are protein molecules that are the very 'glue' that binds extracellular components together. The laminin protein molecule is shaped just like a cross –something that has sparked controversy within the medical and biological world of thinking. Many scientists and medical specialists reject the theory outright and say the findings are just coincidental.[41] If you do take a look at them yourself, as I obviously have, you can make your own mind up. I can sympathise with the deniers on this, but it's difficult not to appreciate that the role and purpose of these structures fits neatly and tidily into a Designer's frame. When you combine the fact they (Laminins) literally hold everything together inside our very bodies, it paints a very interesting picture. Even a cursory reference to Wikipedia, separate of course from any faith-based writings, will show you that.

Laminins are cross-like structures that 'bind to other cell membranes' which 'helps anchor organised tissue to the membrane'. Again, it's difficult not to pick up on claims made in the Bible, this time by Paul, in his letter to the Colossian Church. He says, in Colossians 1:17:

> in Him [Jesus] all things consist.

---

41. www.snopes.com; www.pethos.com (accessed 28.7.20).

The NIV has:

> and in him all things hold together.

In Him (Jesus) all things are held together. I have preached on this verse several times and used the laminin analogy to help explain what this could mean within the very molecular structure of our physical and biological being. I've also used it to show how God sets the earth's cycle so it does not change. Ever since the flood, God's promise is that the seasons would not cease, but keep on following annually, so they could be relied upon. No one back then would have understood the deeper and wider implications of this verse. Only now can we appreciate how amazing this is and remains to be to this day.

> While the earth remains,
> Seedtime and harvest,
> Cold and heat,
> Winter and summer,
> And day and night
> Shall not cease.
> (Genesis 8:22)

This is a remarkable verse of Scripture in itself, as we learn to appreciate that for thousands of years this has remained a constant for us to plant and to sow, to reap and to harvest, to prepare the ground to start again. When you consider before the great flood, seasons would not have existed as there was no rain (Genesis 2:5), it is quite frankly amazing that this has continued and will do so until the end of the present time. The seasons are (scientifically speaking) due to the axis of our earth being tilted at 23.5 degrees, causing variations in seasons, in temperature, light and darkness.

In all these matters, there is a fragile balance that if only a fairly minor disruption occurred, the effects would be devastating. Colossians 1:17 is about more than Laminins of course, but they are, I believe, a pointer, an indicator to the truth of who we are and where we came from. I like to think of us as a masterpiece of God's creation that He has signed, like an original work of art is signed by its creator, or patented by the inventor himself or herself. No one is really looking at the signature. They are transfixed by the painting, the actual 'work of art'. Only after becoming involved in the work of art itself, does one become interested in the painter. Interestingly, the value of the artwork does not come from the materials the artist used, or its subject, but from the authenticity of the artist. Is it really a Picasso? Is it genuinely a Rembrandt? If so, the value becomes almost inestimable. It should, therefore, be of little surprise that God's masterpiece in creation should also be so priceless to Him. That's exactly what we are, and nothing portrays that more or better than when God sent His Son, Jesus Christ to this earth to continue the plan of redemption, during which He would preserve the very pinnacle of His creation: you and I, and all of humankind.

> knowing that you were not redeemed with corruptible things, like silver or gold, from your aimless conduct received by tradition from your fathers, but with the precious blood of Christ, as of a lamb without blemish and without spot. He indeed was foreordained before the foundation of the world, but was manifest in these last times for you who through Him believe in God, who raised Him from the dead and gave Him glory, so that your faith and hope are in God.
> (1 Peter 1:18-21)

15. The Language of Technology

> But you, Daniel, shut up the words, and seal the book until the time of the end; many shall run to and fro, and knowledge shall increase.
> (Daniel 12:4)

The words of the prophet Daniel in the Old Testament are particularity interesting. As for knowledge increasing, an item on the *Digital Journal* website noted this staggering trend:

> Until year 1900, human knowledge approximately doubled every century. However, by 1950 human knowledge doubled every 25 years. In 2000, human knowledge would double every year. Now, our knowledge is almost doubling every day.[42]

Considering the above, have you ever wondered where it will all end? I mean, with technology. It's simply incredible what we can do now in terms of the technology we've created. From robotic, laser microsurgery procedures to 3D printing and nanotechnology. It appears there is no limit. Or is there?

In terms of medicine and medical treatment, I'm a little frustrated at how it has lagged way behind the breakthroughs in commercial and business technology. When it comes to warfare, it seems that 'conflict' is a priority for investment when you compare it with that of other fields. Maybe the role of pharmaceutical companies has complicated and held back development, in their attempt to be financially successful. Apparently now we have the technology

---

42. Taken from Tim Sandle 'Knowledge doubles almost every day, and it's set to increase', www.digitaljournal.com 23 November 2018 (accessed 7.6.20).

to manufacture driverless cars. (The thought of which completely appals me personally as I enjoy driving far too much.) The electric revolution has begun in the car industry (though I'm still baffled as to where all this 'power' to run, charge and maintain the industry is going to come from, let alone the manufacturing and safe disposal of batteries). I'm sure the experts have their answers. We can send satellites into space in order to broadcast images all around the world to communicate, bring live news, show live sport and events as they're happening. We can search the ocean's depths by remote-controlled vessels, fly gigantic aircraft right around the world, conduct space projects beyond yesterday's most vivid imagination, yet we still cannot cure cancer or motor neurone disease, dementia and other incurable illnesses. There's my frustration, right there. Both my parents died of dementia some years ago, but it still rankles with me. It does show, there is some way to go before we see breakthroughs in medicine.

Here's twelve things we still cannot do:

1. Cure dementia
2. Cure many forms of terminal cancer
3. Cure motor neurone disease
4. Cure coronavirus
5. Avoid growing old
6. Avoid death
7. Know the future lottery numbers
8. Teleport from one place to another
9. Change the seasons
10. Stem the growth of the world's population
11. Control the weather
12. Know the future (with any degree of certainty).

You could probably add many more things to this list. Some of these, no doubt eventually we'll get there. The biggest advancement in technology has without doubt been with the internet. It really is a phenomenon. I still remember one of my church members coming to see me about this thing called 'the internet'. It was like listening to someone using a completely foreign language. She spoke of a modem and mobile phones being linked. My first mobile phone looked like a brick, it was so big!

I'm going to take you on a brief bit of time travel now. The prophet Daniel, whom I quoted at the beginning of this chapter, was told by God, that in the last days, or 'time of the end' – 'many shall run to and fro, and knowledge shall increase'.

One might say that this has a certain amount of obviousness about it. The interesting part for me is that it does specify when this prophecy is framed: the 'time of the end'. The prophecy also shows the scenario we see today in our modern world. The advances we've made over a relatively short period of time are nothing short of astronomical. Let's take a closer look.

Invention of photography: 1827
Refrigeration process: 1850s
Industrial steel manufacturing: 1850s
Drilling for oil: 1860
The invention of the telephone by Alexander Bell: 1873
The invention of the motor car: 1880s
The discovery of electricity: 1890s
Invention of air conditioning: 1902
Invention of the aeroplane: 1903
Invention of the radio: 1906
Invention of rocketry: 1926
Invention of the first television set: 1927

Invention of the combine harvester: 1930
Invention of the nuclear bomb: 1939
Invention of the contraception pill: 1960
Invention of the first personal computer: 1970
Invention of the first mobile phone: 1973
Invention of the internet: 1983
Invention of Google: 1998

Breakthrough of DNA via the Human Genome Project 2003

You can easily see from the above, the relatively short time since the 1830s until present day, how in less than 200 years how much knowledge has increased. It is said that 80 per cent of all the world's knowledge has been brought forth over the past ten years. Incredibly 90 per cent of all scientists who have ever lived are alive today. More than a third of the world have smartphones.[43] What a day to be alive!

Public figures such as Elon Musk and the late Stephen Hawking have expressed concerns that 'full artificial intelligence' could result in human extinction. Their concern has led to something called 'singularity'.[44] Simply put, 'singularity' is an 'intelligence explosion' that may (in the experts' opinion) be the possible outcome of us building what is referred to as 'AGI' - Artificial General Intelligence. Again, simply put, this means the ability to produce superhuman machines. This would lead to what is referred to as 'Ultra Intelligent Machines' which have the capability of surpassing the intellectual activities of all or any human being. Personally I do not believe this is possible except by an influence from outside of our world i.e.

43. www.futureoflife.org (accessed 28.7.20).
44. Rory Clellan Jones, 'Stephen Hawking warns artificial intelligence could end mankind', www.bbc.co.uk, 2 December 2014 (accessed 7.6.20).

supernaturally. My belief is that a creator/designer cannot create anything greater than itself. There are many, though, who do believe this is possible and even probable.

'Super intelligence' or 'hyper intelligence', as it's also called, would in many people's opinion be devastatingly destructive. Robin Hanson, professor of economics at George Mason University and an associate at the Future of Humanity Institute at the University of Oxford, is sceptical of such human intelligence augmentation. He believes there will be a slowdown in technology and intelligence once the 'low hanging fruit' of easy methodology for increasing human intelligence is exhausted. Despite this, Hanson goes on to say 'non-human artificial intelligence (also called seed AI) is the most popular option among the hypothesise that would advance an explosion in intelligence'.

Between 1986 and 2007, machines' application-specific capacity to compute information per capita has roughly doubled every fourteen months; the per capita capacity of the world's general-purpose computers has doubled every eighteen months; the global telecommunication capacity per capita doubled every thirty-four months; and the world's storage capacity per capita doubled every forty months. Like other authors, though, Kurzweil reserves the term 'singularity' for a rapid increase in intelligence (as opposed to other technologies), writing for example that 'The Singularity will allow us to transcend these limitations of our biological bodies and brains ... There will be no distinction, post-Singularity, between human and machine'. This information can be found via Ray Kurzweil, an American inventor and futurist. He received the 1999 National Medal of Technology and Innovation from President Bill Clinton. Kurzweil writes that 'there will be no distinction between human and machine'.[45] He also defines his predicted date of singularity to be 2045. This is when he expects computer-based intelligence to significantly exceed the sum total of human brainpower. Some critics, like philosopher Hubert Dreyfus, for instance, assert that computers and/or machines cannot achieve human intelligence. The first scientist to put forward singularity as a plausible possibility was Vernor Vinge in 1993. He wrote, 'within thirty years, we will have the technological means to create superhuman intelligence. Shortly after, the human era will be ended'.[46]

The computer called Deep Blue managed to beat Gary Kasparov (Russian chess grandmaster) in a chess match in 1997. Scientists, philosophers, futurists, and entrepreneurs alike talk about technological evolution. I think this is a strange term, as evolution is supposed to take place in nature, with no external hand to guide it. No creator, inventor or designer is present, yet in the world of technology it seems the rules have to change to suit the mantra. Surely there can be no evolution of computers or machines, only development. It is we, humankind, who are thinking, innovating, inventing, planning our way to what will surely be our last moments of the present day and age. Whenever that may be, it definitely will not happen without designers, scientists, innovators and creative people.

We are on a technological highway which spells danger for us all. Only a global and universal intervention will interrupt this rapidly increasing journey. As I write, we are in the midst of the worst modern era pandemic the world has ever faced. I've just seen a good friend die of the coronavirus, or Covid-19. It is awful and tragic to see so many lives perish across the world. In its wake I hope we can learn to value life more dearly and learn to appreciate not only one another more, but God, our Creator and Designer, too.

---

45. See www.agriville.com (accessed 7.6.20).
46. www.edoras.sdsu.edu (accessed 28.7.20).

The code is getting clearer and clearer by the chapter now. An end is most surely in sight, leading not to super-intelligent machines and computers that we seemingly want to invent, but to a world where the supernatural is natural!

16. The Return of the Nephilim

The 'rise and rise' of technological knowledge might be due to something far more sinister than we ever imagined! After the great flood of Genesis 6, we read that the fallen angels were placed in everlasting chains.

> And the angels who did not keep their proper domain, but left their own abode, He has reserved in everlasting chains under darkness for the judgment of the great day ...
> (Jude 1:6)

The scripture also tells us that these beings shall be released for a time at the end of the age. Although these 'beings' in Revelation 9:1-19 are not called angels, they are from the same place that the angels are incarcerated (Jude 1:6 – 2 Peter 2:4). Therefore, fallen angels clearly are not demons, devils, or even unclean spirits (which are with us in this present age). These are none other than the 'sons of God' who 'sang' on the day of creation (Job 38:7).

These 'sons of God' were not human. Humankind had not yet been created at this point. As we have discussed, they were more than likely angelic beings, but certainly high-ranking as the term in the Hebrew is Elohim (plural). This does not in any way equate them with 'El Elyon' – the God of gods, God Almighty, or as the Hebrew language again describes God as, the 'El Shaddai'.

Peter, the disciple of Christ, also writes:

> God did not spare the angels who sinned, but cast them down to hell and delivered them into chains of darkness, to be reserved for judgment ...
> (2 Peter 2:4)

Peter makes it crystal clear that the fallen angels are not actively involved in the affairs of this world at the moment. (Though they will be in the judgements coming soon upon the earth – Revelation 9:1-21.) We will deal with this in the coming chapters.

Many people find it much easier to believe in God than the devil. This is largely because of traditional portrayals of Satan and his hordes having goat-like features, a pointed tail, and looking like dragons and snakes, and the like. But this is part of the craftiness of the serpent himself. He has many faces and really deceitful camouflage. Paul says:

> Satan himself transforms himself into an angel of light.
> (2 Corinthians 11:14)

There has for many years been an erosion of belief in a 'devil', an entity that the Bible portrays as irrevocably evil and hellbent on the total destruction of any semblance of humanity having a personal relationship with their Creator. He has used many methods from evolution, addiction, war, famine, disease, poverty, suicide, depression, abuse, violence, to materialism, secularism and much, much more to prevent humankind from returning to their Creator - in a word: redemption. I highly recommend you read *The Screwtape Letters* (Geoffrey Bles) written in 1942 by C.S. Lewis. I don't think there's a better book to read on the subject of Satan's methods of camouflaging himself.

Belief in God has definitely been eroded in our world, particularly the God of the Bible, Jehovah, the supreme Lord God and Creator of the universe, and belief in Satan even further, and that's ideal for him as he can operate invisibly, without being exposed. A friend of mine was going to fly back to the UK on a well-known airline which, due to the coronavirus, was cancelled. On trying to get his money back on the flight, the airline quoted they are not covered for an 'act of God'. I think this sums up the general attitude to God these days. Even so, 'There are very few atheists on lifeboats.'

The Bible also speaks of other forms of spirit beings. Demons, devils and unclean spirits. Who are these, then, one might ask? My theory is they are the spirits of the post-flood Nephilim. Let me explain. The pre-flood Nephilim's bodies were destroyed in the flood. Their ancestors, the fallen angels and 'sons of God' of Genesis 6 were not destroyed in the flood as evidenced from the scriptures above. The problem is you cannot destroy a spirit! A spirit is an everlasting creature. You can destroy a body, but not a spirit. This is the main reason why it isn't theologically correct to state God died on the cross. Jesus died on the cross and yes, Jesus was and is God. But He, God, is a spirit who has come in the flesh, in the person of Jesus Christ, so He could physically die. If there was no incarnation there could be no physical death that could be redemptive. In other words, it was the sacrifice of perfect flesh, an innocent human being, that was the only way all human beings could be forgiven. My main point here being that the spirit does not die, it lives on. A spirit can be chained, it can be imprisoned and it is subject to God, and His army of angels and celestial beings who carry God's supreme authority, but it does not die, i.e. cease to exist.

Regarding the demons, devils and unclean spirits, there are several clues in the Gospels as to who and where they came from. They were not created by God,[47] but came about through the wickedness and rebellion of the fallen angels. They were a procreated race, a hybrid species, part divine and part human. In the Gospel of Mark, we read of a man called Legion who derived his name from the devils (demon) that had entered him. Legion, a demon-possessed man,

47 These entities are a by-product of rebellion and sin through Genesis 6. They are the procreated offspring of the illicit union of the sons of God with the daughters of man. These are the spirits of such beings.

living among the tombs in a place called Gadara, on the east side of Galilee. Jesus meets Legion and on seeing Him, is met with a plea from the demons.

> When he saw Jesus from afar, he ran and worshiped Him. And he cried out with a loud voice and said, 'What have I to do with You, Jesus, Son of the Most High God? I implore You by God that You do not torment me.'
> (Mark 5:6-7)

This event is a well-known one amongst Bible scholars. What it shows is the devils within him had a fear of Jesus and did not want Him to 'torment' him / them. The demons speak in both the singular to the plural, probably because the chief demon is speaking on behalf of all of them. He begged Jesus to not send them out of the country:

> For He said to him, 'Come out of the man, unclean spirit!' Then He asked him, 'What is your name?' And he answered, saying, 'My name is Legion; for we are many.' Also he begged Him earnestly that He would not send them out of the country.
> (Mark 5:8-10)

'He' begged Him (Jesus) to not send 'them' out of the country. Then they ask Jesus to send them to the swine, 'that we may enter them' (verse 11). It is clear here that it was preferable for the demons to have a body to possess than none at all. Even being in the pigs was better than being disembodied spirits.

Jesus grants them their wish, knowing full well what will happen. About 2,000 swine are suddenly inhabited by these demons/unclean spirits. The pigs went crazy and all ran over the cliff edge into the Sea of Galilee at one of its deepest points. They were all drowned in the sea. This was 'a masterclass' by Jesus, as to be thrown into the sea like this would've been a huge torment to them and a direct reminder of the flood which either destroyed their bodies or, if they were post-flood Nephilim, their ancestors' bodies.

The Gospel of Luke records a slightly different slant on this.

> And they begged Him that He would not command them to go out into the abyss.
> (Luke 8:31)

The abyss is the very residence of the fallen angels and Nephilim ancestors. They are bound in this place, also referred to as 'Tartarus' (the pit) in 2 Peter 2:4. It is also the 'bottomless pit' referred to in Revelation 9:1. We will look at this in more detail in Chapter 21.

Jesus also taught something else about demons, devils and unclean spirits.

> When an unclean spirit goes out of a man, he goes through dry places, seeking rest; and finding none, he says, 'I will return to my house from which I came.' And when he comes, he finds it swept and put in order. Then he goes and takes with him seven other spirits more wicked than himself, and they enter and dwell there; and the last state of that man is worse than the first.
> (Luke 11:24-26)

Something quite fascinating here is that Jesus refers to the demons' (unclean spirits') desire and prefer their habitat to be as 'dry places'. This can be interpreted as the 'desert places' and fits with Old Testament references to the same.

Post-flood Nephilim are not as powerful as pre-flood Nephilim. Remember that as the Nephilim sired their own sons and daughters, the celestial gene pool weakened through the generations. The terrestrial gene pool grew stronger. This accounts for the mighty men, giants that could be killed by Joshua and David in particular – for example, Goliath. In Jesus' time, the pre-flood Nephilim spirits (if they were not imprisoned along with the fallen angels) would have been the most powerful of the Nephilim. An encounter Jesus had with someone possessed with a devil shows a possible example.

> When Jesus saw that the people came running together, He rebuked the unclean spirit, saying to it, 'Deaf and dumb spirit, I command you, come out of him and enter him no more!' Then the spirit cried out, convulsed him greatly, and came out of him. And he became as one dead, so that many said, 'He is dead.' But Jesus took him by the hand and lifted him up, and he arose. And when He had come into the house, His disciples asked Him privately, 'Why could we not cast it out?' So He said to them, *'This kind can come out by nothing but prayer and fasting.'*
> (Mark 9:25-29, my italics)

This is the only time Jesus makes a distinction between the authority level of devils (demons). But it is very clear that there is one. I set before you that this was either a Nephilim spirit who was pre-flood, or a Nephilim who was an early offspring of the new race of hybrid beings on earth after the flood (post-flood Nephilim). These beings have been around for many years and first came into focus early after the Hebrews left Egypt and prepared to go into the Promised Land (Canaan).

> They sacrificed to demons, not to God,
> To gods they did not know,
> To new gods, new arrivals
> That your fathers did not fear.
> (Deuteronomy 32:17)

This verse pertains to Israel, when they were en route to the Promised Land of Canaan. Israel knew all about the gods of Egypt, but nothing of the 'new gods' of the Canaanites, the Nephilim gods spoken of in Genesis 6. Once in the Promised Land, things changed and the Israelites began to mingle with the Canaanites and to worship their gods too (Psalm 106:35-38).

The Psalms go on to say how the people of God defiled themselves by their own works and polluted the land. Here we basically have unclean spirits who hide behind the idols of gold, silver, bronze, wood and clay. They in themselves (idols) are nothing, but they become objects of worship. So the demons, unclean spirits of the Nephilim, assume their identities and become deities that are worshipped. Paul refers to this in his letter to the Church at Corinth.

> Observe Israel after the flesh: Are not those who eat of the sacrifices partakers of the altar? What am I saying then? That an idol is anything, or what is offered to idols is anything? Rather, that the things which the Gentiles sacrifice they sacrifice to demons and not to God, and I do not want you to have fellowship with demons.
> (1 Corinthians 10:18-20)

So, it is clear what the apostle Paul is saying here. And so it has always been. People often innocently worship false gods and don't realise what they are doing, and more to the point, who they are inviting into their lives. This is why idolatry is such a dangerous thing.

To conclude our chapter, it would appear the Nephilim spirits are still with us. They possess superhuman power and superintelligence handed down to them from their forefathers. They also have different strengths and powers, and no doubt, a hierarchy exists between them, in terms of authority and area of activity. The fallen angels who rebelled against Almighty God being still in chains, it is the

Nephilim who are managing Satan's rule of evil upon the earth at the moment. The ancestors of the Nephilim spirits (fallen angels) are only in chains for a season. There is a time coming very soon when they will be released upon the the earth. They will wreak great havoc in the world.

Hopefully you will see something that makes sense of all that mythology in past folklore now, of aliens and UFOs and of ghosts and spirits. These are all expressions of the Nephilim spirits who have a supernatural capability as they themselves are genetically hybrids of terrestrial flesh and celestial flesh. The presence of powerful Nephilim spirits upon the face of the earth will bring new phenomenal revelation and superintelligence. This will be downloaded to us, constantly bringing answers to mysteries for a long time unfathomed and unexplained. These spirits also bring with them brutality and sadistic practices similar to those that used to be practised before the world was flooded. Remember, God did not flood the whole world because humanity was sinful and rebellious, self-seeking, proud and disobedient. He destroyed the world because of the introduction of 'strange flesh', even like in Sodom and Gomorrah, where some of the men of that city lusted after 'strange flesh' (Jude 1:7). So much more, far-reaching wickedness ensued.

The point has been made several times in *Code Red* so I will not repeat myself, but to underline exactly how important and serious this was to God, the following warning therefore must also be taken seriously. Jesus said:

> But of that day and hour no one knows, not even the angels of heaven, but My Father only. *But as the days of Noah were, so also will the coming of the Son of Man be.* For as in the days before the flood, they were eating and drinking, marrying and giving in marriage, until the day that Noah entered the ark,

> and did not know until the flood came and took them all away,
> so also will the coming of the Son of Man be.
> (Matthew 24:36-39, my italics)

To conclude this chapter before we begin our countdown to the end of the age, the salutary warning is abundantly clear. Jesus says that the spiritual environment at the time of the end of the age will be exactly the same as it was just before the flood. The Church has preached for 2,000 years that the Lord is coming. And so He is, sooner than many think.

17. The Ticking Time Bomb

The mental health dilemma

In all areas of life, I believe the battlefield is the mind. Whether it's sport, career, marriage, leisure, it's about the mind. The book of Proverbs says of a man, 'as he thinks in his heart, so is he' (Proverbs 23:7).

As I write, I've just heard of a celebrity who used to present a well-known 'reality' TV series called *Love Island*. She took her own life due to struggling with mental health issues. A beautiful, successful, glamorous woman who had fame, fortune and so much to live for, Caroline Flack was only forty years of age. She simply couldn't take any more of the bullying she received from those on social media, the press and the CPS (Crown Prosecution Service) whom, it appears, had taken the decision to go ahead and prosecute her for an altercation she had with her boyfriend. It seems in the aftermath of this tragedy, that all parties set about to find somebody to blame.

Unfortunately, this is typical of the world in which we now live. It has become so much easier to attack people from the safety of our own homes, often anonymously and ruthlessly, without fear of the damage we may cause. I've been on the receiving end of accusations and horrible verbal assaults and there's hardly anything you can do to respond effectively. Self-defence is virtually impossible!

The ticking time bomb of poor mental health has already exploded for many. Others are currently battling with mental struggles, sometimes in complete silence. I watched on YouTube[48] recently how the boxer Tyson Fury shared his own experiences of mental health problems. He constantly fought with himself, probably far harder than any opponent in the ring, to overcome negative and suicidal thoughts, alcohol and on occasions even took drugs. Again,

48. https://YouTube.be/ITLlbs4cOX4 (accessed 7.6.20).

an incredibly successful, famous and now wealthy sportsman with a wonderful wife and family around him, couldn't overcome the demons of the mind as some have described this personal battlefield.

I, too, have had my own deep and dark days throughout well over three decades of full-time ministry. I've had to constantly fight what is now called 'imposter syndrome', a condition when you don't feel 'the right' to be in the company of your colleagues and peers. This has plagued me all through most of my ministry. The more successful I was deemed to have become, building a great church and far-reaching ministry, the less worthy I felt to be the leader of that particular church and ministry.

My full story is told in my first book *The Rubicon* (meaning a place of no return) in which I chart the small beginnings I inherited with a tiny church in Chorlton, south Manchester. I had to learn that God's grace is more than sufficient to bring me through and to stand in that position of God's grace and favour, not because I was worthy, not because I was good at doing what I did, but because the Bible said He is with me and will continue to be with me (Matthew 28:20). I think our 'call' is sometimes much stronger than our 'gifting'. I continue to claim that truth in times of great insecurity and self-doubt.

At one point the syndrome was so bad, I chose not to mix with successful people or some of my peers, because of my past. My education was nothing short of a disaster. No PhD, no degree, no academic credibility.

In one year, we saw 70-80 per cent growth numerically in the church. Also, a high percentage of the growth was new conversion, but this only ever added to the feeling that I wasn't deserving, somehow, of God's blessing, let alone the acceptance of my peers. I should add here I have many colleagues and peers who are incredibly successful and well-known who have only ever embraced me with love and acceptance.

We all go through things that are extremely difficult to explain and quantify. By the way, I'm much better now with this, as I've learned how to deal with it all.

Poor mental health can affect anyone, irrespective of age, gender, wealth, background, social status, success or religion. Yes, it happens in church life too. Pastors, church leaders are not exempt or immune from poor mental health issues.

'Poor mental health' is a description of the state of our mental well-being. We all have mental health, the same as we have physical health. With poor physical health, we can at least understand it far more easily and get to know what to do about it. Poor mental health goes largely under the radar. Who would ever thought that some of the funniest men in the world struggled with depression and anxiety? Robin Williams and Tommy Cooper both had their battles with mental health issues. Maybe they learned to hide their troubles behind their humour. Behind their smiles and laughter lay a darkened world of depression and poor mental well-being. It's very hard to explain that.

In India we have homes full of children orphaned by parents who chose to end their own lives. But this is different, I believe, as the trigger for these actions is usually a bad experience. A parent loses all their wealth, possessions and job and has no way to support their family. A wife is abandoned by her husband, for another woman. She is left without hope, without a future in a culture that does not respect single mothers. A farmer loses his tenancy through debt and knows there's only one way out of the hopelessness and despair he feels. A boy or girl (or both) end their lives because the caste system – and, consequently, their parents – do not allow their marriage. These cases are tragic, but they are common and a different situation to the one of poor mental health. I believe we are witnessing a mental 'mind explosion' as we have gone beyond what is healthy for our minds in terms of the way we live our lives today.

Recently, many businesses stopped hiring staff on the basis of their IQ. Instead, they hire on the basis of their EQ. EQ, stands for 'emotional quotient'.[49] This is a person's ability to manage their emotional lives in a positive way, so as to relieve stress, communicate without anxiety and bring rationale into those moments of panic and stressful challenge. Our emotional well-being is essential to our mental well-being. Literally, how we feel – what our mood is like. Are we balanced, and calm under pressure? Do we understand our own selves well? We are finely and intricately made. Here are several things that I believe are paramount in our chemical make-up that enable our moods and our emotions to be both positive and healthy.

Our physical health

Our physical health is connected closely to our emotional health and well-being.

1. *Bodily exercise.* This is not just good for the body, it's good for the mind and soul too. It is now known that exercise releases certain endorphins into our bloodstream that are incredibly influential to our mood and emotional feelings. These endorphins are strategically secreted into the brain via physical exercise and activate the body's opiate receptors that help bring about a feeling of pleasure, satisfaction and contribute greatly to our general well-being.

49. See 'The importance of Emotional Intelligence in the workplace', www.ciphr.com; 'Emotional Intelligence counts for twice as much as IQ and technical skills combined in determining who will be a top performer', www.businessnewsdaily.com (accessed 28.7.20). www.higheredjobs.com reported many hiring managers (71%) stated they valued EI (also referred to as EQ) over IQ and (59%) claim they'd pass up a candidate with a high IQ but low emotional intelligence (accessed 28.7.20).

2. *Rest and recuperation.* It's vital that our bodies get the right amount of rest. Rest helps to heal and re-energise us, ready for the demands of the day on our minds and our emotions. If we don't get enough rest, it will affect our mood greatly.

3. *Leisure activities.* This is bigger than many people think. I meet a number of people who have little leisure in their lives. It's actually not that they're too busy. It's because they don't 'make time' for that kind of stuff. Many are workaholics and don't realise the importance of the saying 'a change is as good as a rest', but that's the reality. In many ways, golf saved my mental well-being! I used to play loads of football, which enabled me to mix with people much younger than I am. This was great for me at the time. Once my old anterior cruciate ligament injury kicked in again at about thirty-eight years old, it was time to stop playing, or I'd have to stop walking or doing anything active! I chose to take up golf at forty years of age and it's been a life-saver. It's one of the greatest ways to get your mind off the day-to-day pressure and stress. Find a hobby, a pursuit, a pastime, whether it's stamp collecting, gardening, snooker, ten-pin bowling, fishing, golf or whatever. Leisure time is a time of release. A time of refreshing. Try it! Find something you enjoy and just do it.

Our emotional relationships

1. *Our soul mates.* We are not created to do life alone. Whilst I enjoy ample amounts of solitude, good friends are as important to our emotional well-being as oxygen is to our bodies. Our soul mates are those who 'get' us, and we 'get' them. Value these relationships greatly. Invest in them with your time, energy, money. Learn the importance of 'kindred spirits' I have a few of these people in my life and I treasure them.

2. *Our life partner.* This should be our wife, our husband, the one person we have chosen to spend our life with. The happiest people on the planet are those with a great relationship with one outstanding individual. My wife of thirty-four years is exactly this to me. My best friend, lover, confidant, supporter, critic and companion.

3. *Our wider social relationships.* Mates, friends, pals, relationships of a completely different kind but oh, so important. My friends: we talk together, eat together, play together, golf together at times and have fun together. They may not necessarily be as close as the other relationships I've mentioned, but they're vital in their own way. Interactive, social relationships are massively important for our well-being.

4. *Working relationships.* Work colleagues, team members, relationships that are purposeful and centre around working towards a goal. These relationships are yet another strand of wholesomeness to enable us to continue to grow and develop our character and our personality. This is one of the reasons why unemployment is such a curse. It limits our development, our community involvement and restricts any influence we might have too.

Our relationship with ourselves

It seems strange to say it, but the way we relate to ourselves is also very important. There are times when we feel good about ourselves and other times, not so good. Certain aspects of ourselves we may dislike a lot. So our self-image can be poor and our self-awareness becomes too 'emphasised' as a result, making us feel, in turn, uncomfortable, nervous or edgy. We need to realise that being around our work colleagues and our friends is always an opportunity to learn more about ourselves and become better people.

So... learn to handle yourself in your routines. How much sleep you need (and this may change greatly as you get older). What chemicals you allow in your body. What you eat and drink. Are there certain vitamins you can take that will help you? Poor mental health can easily be the result of chemical imbalance. Natural ingredients and supplements such as ginger, turmeric, walnuts, fish oil, fruits, especially red fruits with good amounts of antioxidants in them. It's safe to test and trial these things. Honey too is an excellent natural product, especially non-blended varieties.

Relationship with places

Sounds funny, I know, but we should all have at least one 'happy place'. I have several. One of them is India in the middle of the jungle. I absolutely love being there. It feeds my soul and refreshes my spirit. It's a bit far to go, though, so something nearer is needed! I have another place in the Lake District. And, of course, my garden, which whilst not huge, is a sanctuary and refuge. I have a beautiful log cabin aka 'man cave' in my garden, where I write, pray and sometimes do nothing but think, pray and do some crosswords to keep my mind alert, and try to keep my vocabulary stretched. I prayer-journal too, something I've done for about twenty-plus years now.

My last piece of advice to you to help you along the way, is: find something much bigger than you and give yourself to it. Sometimes volunteering for a charity can be pure medicine. Help the homeless, volunteer in a charity shop, help with their admin – this list is as long as you make it. *Realise this: someone, somewhere needs you.*

How does all this relate to Code Red, I hear some of you saying? Well, I believe it is a vital sign of things going into meltdown as the world/society begins to react to the pace of life and technology as a whole. One of the biblical signs of the times is that 'men's hearts [will fail] them from fear and the expectation of those things which are coming on the earth, for the powers of the heavens will be shaken' (Luke 21:26). That doesn't need to be you. If you're forewarned you can become forearmed, ready to face those moments that are about to come upon the earth as 'signs' of the end of the age.

As I write, we are right in the middle of the coronavirus pandemic. It is utterly unbelievable how such a potentially lethal new virus can cause such panic and mayhem upon the earth. But it has! Our whole church has had to go into complete lockdown as far as our gatherings are concerned. All our services now have to be streamed live online, instead of people attending in person, for fear of catching the virus. What I'm saying throughout this book is real, and it is a warning to everyone. Make sure you understand God's plan of redemption for you and your family. Just like Noah and his family.

In the light of all the above, let's look at taking our mental health into being our mental wealth.

Remember what we said at the beginning of this chapter? The battlefield is the mind. If you win there, you can win anywhere.

Lastly, be careful who you let into your inner circle of friends, and those you allow yourself to become connected to. Toxic relationships need to be replaced with healthy ones. If you can, phase them out of your life. If you can't phase them out, cut them out, as your future mental well-being may very well depend on it. If you can't do it, speak to a close confidant to help you to do it.

Be careful how you help 'hurt' people. Of course, 'hurt' people need helping. But be aware – 'hurt people, hurt people'; they can suck the very life out of you if you allow it. They may not even be aware of it. These kinds of relationships can drain you dry, leaving you mentally and emotionally exhausted. Do not allow that to happen.

> You [God] will keep him in perfect peace,
> Whose mind is stayed on You,
> Because he trusts in You.
> (Isaiah 26:3)

Other great guidelines gleaned from other sources

Self-management. You're able to control impulsive feelings and behaviours, manage your emotions in healthy ways, take initiative, follow through on commitments, and adapt to changing circumstances.

Self-awareness. You recognise your own emotions and how they affect your thoughts and behaviour. You know your strengths and weaknesses, and have self-confidence.

Social awareness. You have empathy. You can understand the emotions, needs and concerns of other people, pick up on emotional cues, feel comfortable socially, and recognise the power dynamics in a group or organisation.

Relationship management. You know how to develop and maintain good relationships, communicate clearly, inspire and influence others, work well in a team, and manage conflict.

These are great guidelines on how to manage ourselves and make our own self-assessments on our own mental well-being. I also would recommend the book *Didn't See it Coming* by Carey Niewhof.[50] This is the story of an incredibly successful pastor in Canada who just 'hit the wall' in his own life. His recorded experience will prove enormously useful to anyone in any form of leadership struggling with their own mental health issues.

---

50. Carey Niewhof, *Didn't See It Coming* (Colorado Springs, CO: WaterBrook Press, 2018).

18. A New Normal

> Woe those who call evil good, and good evil;
> Who put darkness for light, and light for darkness;
> Who put bitter for sweet, and sweet for bitter!
> (Isaiah 5:20)

Earlier in the book, I talked about boundaries. Today we have already removed the ancient boundaries of our forefathers in many areas of life. We are now being told quite candidly and blatantly, in the Western world especially, that a new set of 'norms' is being set out for us all. New social values are being fostered and adopted for future generations to come, whether we agree with them or not. Landmark, traditional values and biblical viewpoints are being brushed aside and no longer tolerated in this new era of 'tolerance'. Tolerance has itself become totally subjective. Whose tolerance? It depends on who's setting the agenda. As long as we don't adhere to new values being set for us, and adopt new societal values, we are classed as intolerant and bigoted. If we dare to put our heads above the parapet, and express traditional biblical views, we are in danger of being accused of 'hate speech'. For many of us, born in the 1950s and 1960s, this represents a sea change in society.

Every traditional belief and opinion is now being constantly challenged. Belief in the sanctity of marriage being binary, between a man and a woman, issues around gender, transgender, sexuality, are obvious standout examples that now have 'new norms'. There is no leeway, it seems, for any compromise on these views. The freedom to choose one's own belief system is being denied in countries around the world today; views that once championed free speech and true democracy. Everything, it appears, is open to question and to change.

My own belief and opinion is that marriage is sacred in the eyes of God, as set out in the Bible (Genesis 2:24).[51] I know this binary view is no longer deemed acceptable, but it is still mine. Even some evangelical leaders, some of them very well-known and reputable, have changed their stance on the matter of sexuality and gender. I can see that some of these changes have been made due to pressures made upon them by their peers and their sponsors and, of course, the main drivers of the new norms, the media. That which used to be normal is now abnormal and unacceptable. That which used to be abnormal and unacceptable is now the opposite. For my part, I'm very clear. I am for total tolerance in society. I believe with all my heart that no one should be forced to believe in a particular opinion when it comes to faith and personal belief. Everyone is entitled to their own personal faith and belief, as long as it does not lead to violence and aggressive behaviour towards any individual. But tolerance has to be a two-way street and not a one-way, six-lane highway.

To hold one's beliefs in God and the Bible in a traditional manner is now susceptible to all types of discrimination and prejudice. I know of people dismissed from their jobs in the UK just for questioning TV programmes on social media platforms with regard to homosexuality, for instance. Another was suspended from work for praying for a dying person. No doubt a time is coming when an attempt to force pastors and church leaders to conduct same-sex marriages will come, even though we were told this would not happen. There are clergy who will happily bless and conduct same-sex marriages, but that won't be enough for those driving the 'new normal' agenda.

I believe the time is coming soon where pastors and church leaders will be sentenced to prison for refusing to conduct gay marriages. This is the landscape we are moving into rapidly. Many churches will lose their Gift Aid, charitable status, as they will be labelled 'non-compliant'

51. See Titus 1:6; also Matthew 19:4-6; 1 Timothy 3:2; 1 Peter 3:7.

with the government or state. Banks will refuse to do business with some churches on the same basis. Even advertising companies will refuse to do business with traditional, evangelical churches. Nurses and teachers will be summarily dismissed, policemen and women too. We know politicians aren't allowed traditional views without going through a 'media hell' and questioning worthy of the Spanish Inquisition! Hotels will refuse bookings to blacklisted Christians and their credit ratings will be jeopardised. These things will be expedited via the one-world mechanism coming to all of us in the coming days. I will deal with this in a later chapter.

When we used to have an extensive ministry in Romania, we encountered similar stories. This was especially so amongst our Dunamis Youth Camp. We came up against so many governmental and commercial organisations who point-blank refused to work with us, just because we were labelled '*pocaiti*' – literally, 'repented ones'. This stigma against Christians still remains to this day. I cannot for the life of me understand why this should be the case, as 'repentance' is at the core and foundation of the Christian message per se. The traditional churches have this at the heart of their creed.

As I've already said, as I write this, we're in the middle of a lockdown here in the UK. Yesterday, I went to the post office to pick up a package (as I'm allowed to do – with social distancing, of course). I couldn't believe my eyes as I parked my car in a well-known supermarket car park and witnessed all the shoppers queuing up 2m apart to comply with government rules. It was like watching a dystopian sci-fi film. It's another new normal! The coronavirus effect is creating many new norms. Easter Sunday has just passed by. We've just done church online as we cannot meet physically. On Good Friday, we had communion together via satellite. We are having all our meetings on the Zoom video platform, another new normal. Shaking hands has been replaced by and elbow bump or a '*namaste*'

(Hindi for 'welcome'). New normals are springing up everywhere. I actually think this Covid-19 season will change the world in which we live, forever. Social distancing, online meetings and deals are going to become new norms too.

It is obvious that we are living in a rapidly changing world where we are becoming more and more secular in nature. I think, though, that this will change as people experience an emptiness that only the Creator can fill; a void in which only a personal relationship with our Creator can truly reside, enabling us to feel more at peace with ourselves, our fellow human beings and the world we live in.

Of course, Jesus spoke about there being two ways. A broad way and a narrow way. Many will find the broad way, but few will find the narrow way (Matthew 7:13-14). This obviously means the narrow way is not the most popular choice, but it is the right way and the true way. The code of redemption means we must choose the right way. That won't be easy, but it definitely will be worth it. We also need to be wise in what we embrace as new norms in our lives. It would be very easy to compromise and go with the flow, but as someone once pointed out, healthy fish oxygenate themselves and clean their gills out when they swim against the tide. Dead fish and sickly fish flow with the current, not against it.

My aim here is not to decry all change, and there are some great new norms – I've adopted some myself. Many of them have come from a desire to develop personally as a leader and to grow as a Christian, but they must come from choices and self-discipline. No one can do that for us; only we ourselves can do that.

I began this chapter with a verse in the Bible where God gave a salutary warning about those who 'call evil good, and good evil; Who put darkness for light, and light for darkness' (Isaiah 5:20).

This is the place I fear we have come to now in society. We have slowly moved from tolerance to acceptance, and from acceptance to propagation of opposite values and belief systems in our world. This has become quite worrying for many. It has also become obvious to many ordinary folk, but seemingly not to our leaders, politically and socially. Even many religious leaders, Christian and other faiths, have abandoned their traditional bases, adapting to more modern and so-called 'progressive views', and seem to be hellbent on setting this agenda for all of us. However, the agenda is not really being driven by people. It is being driven by 'principalities' and 'powers' (Ephesians 6:12) that are very real but not visible. It is called the anti-Christian agenda and it is coming from the spirit of Antichrist spoken of in 2 Thessalonians 2:7:

> For the mystery of lawlessness is already at work; only He who now restrains will do so until He is taken out of the way.

This scripture shows two things. Firstly, that the lawlessness at the end of the age will be a 'mystery'. i.e. it is not logical, it doesn't make sense. We are right here now. We cannot grasp how people are becoming a) more critical b) more rebellious c) more disobedient in terms of criminality and lawlessness. We don't exactly know why, but most of us, if not nearly all of us, would agree it is getting worse, not better. Secondly, there is a restraining force. There has always been speculation as to who 'He' refers to here, but 'He' is described as the restrainer. And 'He' shall be 'taken out of the way'. Some Bible scholars say it's the Church, which is called to be 'salt' and 'light' in the world (Matthew 5:13-16). Others say it is the Holy Spirit. I'm heavily inclined to agree with the latter as the define article in the scripture 'He' is masculine and not feminine. The Church has always been referred to as feminine. The bride, 'she' not 'He'. Also, we must remember that the Holy Spirit is not an 'it' but a 'He'. He is God, just like the Father is God and the Son also is God.

The Holy Spirit is the One who started the Church age, at Pentecost some 2,000 years ago. He came to replace Jesus in presence, in word and in deed. Here Jesus states and affirms this truth in the gospel of John:

> But now I go away to Him who sent Me, and none of you asks Me, 'Where are You going?' But because I have said these things to you, sorrow has filled your heart. Nevertheless I tell you the truth. It is to your advantage that I go away; for if I do not go away, the *Helper* will not come to you; but if I depart, I will send *Him* to you. And when *He* has come, *He* will convict the world of sin, and of righteousness, and of judgment: of sin, because they do not believe in Me; of righteousness, because I go to My Father and you see Me no more; of judgment, because the ruler of this world is judged. I still have many things to say to you, but you cannot bear them now. However, when *He*, *the Spirit of truth*, has come, *He* will guide you into all truth; for *He* will not speak on His own authority, but whatever *He* hears *He* will speak; and *He* will tell you things to come. *He* will glorify Me, for *He* will take of what is Mine and declare it to you. All things that the Father has are Mine. Therefore I said that *He* will take of Mine and declare it to you.
> (John 16:5-15, my italics)

So because Jesus ascended to heaven after His resurrection, the Holy Spirit came in His place to be the One who empowers, and enables faith in our hearts to arise and be witnesses to the truth of Jesus' message. Jesus Himself predicted this shortly before His ascension.

> But you shall receive power when the *Holy Spirit* has come upon you; and you shall be witnesses to Me in Jerusalem, and in all Judea and Samaria, and to the end of the earth.
> (Acts 1:8, my italics)

So, you can clearly see here, the message and the mission. It has remained the same for generations until this day. The message is one of redemption, and is the main reason for writing this book. The mission is to reach as many people as is possible in all the world before the end of this present age. For, believe me, that time is fast approaching, and we need to understand the message. It is coded, it is red and it is real.

We now start to draw to the end of *Code Red.* Some things are only conjecture and interpretation, but other major things are factual and are about to be unveiled upon our world and in our time.

19. Welcome to Your Own Biochip

We now come to one of the most challenging prophecies in the Bible for us in the last days. It is found in the last book, the book of Revelation. This book has often been shrouded in mystery and differences of opinion, even in the way we should read it. For myself, I believe we should read it with a few golden rules. Firstly, I believe there is much typology in it that we should not present as literal. However, secondly, much of the typology is used to describe literal events, so care must be taken to differentiate between the two. Thirdly, everything in the book has to be examined in the light of already revealed Scripture and the writings of the apostles who have prepared the road, so to speak, to the apostle John's writings.

We are going to go right to the middle of the book for our introduction into what the Bible describes as a cashless society. Revelation 13 shows a world leader arise who is ruthless and tyrannical. He will bring in a one world order and system that is made mandatory for all the people of the world. Let's take a closer look.

> Then I saw another beast coming up out of the earth, and he had two horns like a lamb and spoke like a dragon. And he exercises all the authority of the first beast in his presence, and causes the earth and those who dwell in it to worship the first beast, whose deadly wound was healed. He performs great signs, so that he even makes fire come down from heaven on the earth in the sight of men. And he deceives those who dwell on the earth by those signs which he was granted to do in the sight of the beast, telling those who dwell on the earth to make an image to the beast who was wounded by the sword and lived. He was granted power to give breath to the image of the beast, that the image of the beast should both speak and

> cause as many as would not worship the image of the beast to be killed. He causes all, both small and great, rich and poor, free and slave, to receive a mark on their right hand or on their foreheads, and that no one may buy or sell except one who has the mark or the name of the beast, or the number of his name. Here is wisdom. Let him who has understanding calculate the number of the beast, for it is the number of a man: His number is 666.
> (Revelation 13:11-18)

Note how those who refuse to be part of this system are prevented from buying or selling – their economic capability is taken away completely. This is already very much in the pipeline. Very recently, in July of 2018, thousands of Swedes consented to having microchips fitted under their skin to aid them with making financial transactions. Biohax International has already pioneered this system. I encourage you to google 'Biohax' yourself. They're on Facebook and Twitter @biohaxint. Their bio speaks of themselves as a 'Global leader in biochip implants'. So, in actual fact I'm not actually saying 'it's coming' – I'm saying 'it's already here'. Many of the country's gyms are already equipped to recognise biochips as passcodes.[52]

The scripture however gives us a slight glimmer of guidance in verse 18. The recognition of the beast's economic strategy can be worked out. It can be calculated. The number 666 will be easily identifiable within the whole system and serve as a sign to everyone who has read or heard of this prophecy. Remember these words.

China's social credit system has been in place for years and controls much of the behaviour and movements of many of its citizens. Think of our own economic system. Most of our transactions are rapidly becoming electronic. We were also, it seems, about to enter into a

52. See 'Is Biochipping a Good Idea?' www.fortune.com (accessed 20.4.20).

massive financial contract with Chinese company Huawei. Huawei is a leading (if not the leading) global information and communications technology solutions provider. They were about to do a deal with the UK in which they would introduce their 5G network across the nation. The present coronavirus in the world and particularly in the UK and USA is presenting doubt about the deal. Switzerland banned the 5G giants for six months whilst they did further in-depth research, as they felt there were health issues possibly arising from the use of their phones. We have just heard that the UK decided not to go ahead with the deal with Huawei.

The prophecy of Revelation 13 is literally upon us as I write. The big difference is, it is at the early trial stage. It will, however, come in gently and softly. In reality, it's a great idea. Who, in this day and age, doesn't appreciate the fact that we no longer have to traipse to the local bank to pay in cheques and withdraw cash? On one of my banking apps I already have has the facility to pay in cheques by screen-shooting them with my phone and paying them in on my mobile phone. It's a really convenient tool to have literally in your hand.

The New York Times recently wrote an article about the increase in the influence of technology upon our lives: 'If its use continues to grow and the right regulations aren't instituted, we might lose the ability to go out in public without being recognized by the police, our neighbors and corporations.'[53]

One of the objections is about people's loss of their personal and private freedoms. For instance, most of today's online appliances can trace our movements. When we're at home, when we're out shopping, eating, meeting friends, attending football matches, going to the gym or going to church. Soon, all our movements will be known not just

53. Woodrow Hartzog, Evan Selinger, 'Why You Can No Longer Get Lost in the Crowd', *The New York Times*, 17 April 2019.

to a bank of algorithms, which in a way protect some of your privacy, in that it's not a person but a 'machine', a computer – but the place we're heading towards is far more sinister and contrived. Whilst much of our present-day technology is a great force for good, in the wrong hands it could be nothing short of catastrophic.

Gerard Baker, *The Wall Street Journal*'s editor, stated we have pulled back the curtain regarding the 'benefits' of technology in an April 2019 article titled 'Technology Isn't a Force for Liberation After All'.[54] He wrote:

> In the hands of competent and exploitative forces, such as, let's say, the People's Republic of China or Facebook, the long march toward enslavement by technology continues apace. For all its benefits, artificial intelligence of the sort that drives facial-recognition software and a million other capabilities is proving an extraordinarily useful implement in the furtherance of repression.

Baker goes on to say:

> governments are using AI and other technologies in myriad ways to silence dissent, undermine opponents and promote their own ideologies …
>
> Even during the Arab Spring, technology demonstrated it could be a double-edged sword, with autocratic governments using then-emergent technologies to track and hunt down troublemakers. And now, in less than a decade, advances

54. 'Technology Isn't a Force for Liberation After All', www.wsj.com (accessed 20.4.20).

> have accelerated. China leads the way, but governments of an authoritarian bent are eagerly acquiring and adapting similar tools.

> He continues to say, 'The possibilities are chilling'.

Let's park that for a moment. Once this system is up and running, it will be unified and comprehensively systemised to include the world's population. This will become a massive system of control. China's social credit system is by far the most advanced and well-used in this regard. *The Guardian* describes it this way:

> China's social credit system [is] a big-data system for monitoring and shaping business and citizens' behaviors is reaching beyond China's borders to impact foreign companies, according to new research.
>
> The system, which has been compared to an Orwellian tool of mass surveillance, is an ambitious work in progress: a series of big data and AI-enabled processes that effectively grant subjects a social credit score based on their social, political and economic behaviour. People with low scores can be banned or blacklisted from accessing services including flights and train travel; while those with high scores can access privileges. The Chinese government aims to have all 1.35 billion of its citizens subject to the system by 2020.[55]

We are now in 2020, awaiting the lifting of the lockdown from Covid-19. What better opportunity to see the advantages of a universal system of biochip coding leading to a totally cashless system?

---

55. Kelsey Munro, 'China's Social Credit System "Could Interfere in Other Nations' Sovereignty"', 27 June 2018, www.theguardian.com (accessed 7.6.20).

Business magnate Bill Gates is the latest person to champion the same system in his Event 201 project. Just google Event 201 and it is all there in the open for all to read. Gates has called for a 'Digital Certificate' to help identify anyone who goes on to receive the Covid-19 vaccine. The plan is already backed up by a huge organisation called ID2020. In October of 2019, the Bill & Melinda Gates Foundation, in cooperation with the World Economic Forum (WEF), hosted an Event 201, which included a simulation of a global pandemic. Crazy, but true! Bill Gates himself led a session, which I watched myself, on the need for a system to register people, not just data. It was really convincing, making a lot of sense. Gates also referred to the ebola virus as an example of being 'behind' in terms of preparedness and readiness to deal with such an outbreak. One of the claims he made was that a new coronavirus could easily wipe out 65 million people, simply because we are unprepared.[56]

Steven Mosher, an internationally recognised authority on China, wrote an article for *The New York Post* entitled: 'China's New "Social Credit System" Is a Dystopian Nightmare'.[57] Think of this! A government system that monitors more than a billion people, tracks every aspect of their lives, and then ranks people with a score and doles out punishments and fines for not acting in accordance with whatever the government decides is right and wrong. And this is not merely hypothetical. The system has already had real-world consequences:

> Would-be air travellers were blocked from buying tickets 17.5 million times last year for 'social credit' offences including

56. www.usatoday.com; www.centreforhealthsecurity.org; www.vigilantcitizen.com (accessed 07.6.20).
57. See 'China's New 'Social Credit System' is a Dystopian Nightmare', 18 May 2019, www.nypost.com (accessed 7.6.20).

> unpaid taxes and fines … Others were banned 5.5 million times from buying train tickets, according to the National Public Credit Information Center.[58]

Mosher's article in *The New York Post* chillingly reported:

> One of the ways that people can improve their own social credit score is to report on the supposed misdeeds of others. Individuals can earn points, for example, for reporting those who violate the new restrictions on religious practice, such as Christians who illegally meet to pray in private homes … Of course, as the state progresses ever closer toward its goal of monitoring all of the activities of its citizens 24 hours a day, seven days a week, society itself becomes a virtual prison.[59]

Incredible statements from very experienced authors and academics.

In a nutshell, once this system becomes mandatory, many people will end up being killed for their refusal to accept the biochip. They will at first be fugitives upon the earth, unable to buy and sell. Their economic situation has been taken from them. They will be unable to gain meaningful employment. They will have to scavenge and forage to stay alive. The book of Revelation indicates there will be many martyrs in this new era. The warning is clear.

> Then a third angel followed them, saying with a loud voice, 'If anyone worships the beast and his image, *and receives his mark*

---

58. Joe McDonald, 'China Bars Millions from Travel for "Social Credit" Offences', 22 February 2019.
59. Steven Mosher, 'China's New 'Social Credit System' Is a Dystopian Nightmare', *The New York Post*, 18 May 2019.

> *on his forehead or on his hand*, he himself shall also drink of the wine of the wrath of God, which is poured out full strength into the cup of His indignation. He shall be tormented with fire and brimstone in the presence of the holy angels and in the presence of the Lamb. And the smoke of their torment ascends forever and ever; and they have no rest day or night, who worship the beast and his image, and whoever receives the mark of his name.
> (Revelation 14:9-11, my italics)

So, it is very clear that this will be a step too far, as far as the Lord has decided. Here's where this book, *Code Red*, becomes a survival manual for the soul! *Do not take this biochip. Do not receive it in your body, whether by tattoo or microchip.* To do so is to cross the line set by God Himself. Many will die because they refuse to have the mark, but their souls will be spared in the final judgement.

> And I saw thrones, and they sat on them, and judgment was committed to them. Then I saw the souls of those who had been beheaded for their witness to Jesus and for the word of God, who had not worshiped the beast or his image, and *had not received his mark on their foreheads or on their hands.* And they lived and reigned with Christ for a thousand years. But the rest of the dead did not live again until the thousand years were finished. This is the first resurrection.
> (Revelation 20:4-5, my italics)

Here we have the confirmation of those who have been martyred for the sake of the witness of Christ Jesus. They 'had not worshiped the beast of his image' and *had refused to take his mark on their foreheads or hands.*

Many people reading this may think this is far-fetched and exaggerated. However, the code of redemption is everywhere we look. We simply cannot have excuses. From the beginning of creation until this very day, God is gracious and merciful, 'not wanting any to perish' (2 Peter 3:9, NRSV), but that all may know Him and have eternal life. That is, when the end comes, we will be raised to a new life, with our own new body, like His own celestial body (Philippians 3:20-21).

Choose redemption instead of damnation. Damnation is following the way of Satan, his fallen angels, the Nephilim spirits and all the hierarchy of the devil. You don't have to go his way. It is a broad way, and it's the easy way, and it may even seem the right way, but it will end in misery, judgement and everlasting punishment. The alternative is to believe on the Lord Jesus Christ, in your heart. Believe God sent His Son to die for us all, and that includes you. Rebellion upon the earth will come to a close. God and His kingdom will overcome. These things are not far-fetched, they are being planned and are coming into play as I write. The coronavirus is providing a new rationale which will help launch a new system, a new global network, that will make millions of people prisoners of another kingdom. That kingdom may seem just like a human one on the surface, but it is far more sinister and far more dangerous than you can imagine.

At the end of this book, I will present you with an exit strategy that means whenever this new era and dictatorship emerges, you can use it to escape the coming judgement and all that entails.

20. The End of Days

The Bible speaks specifically about a period of time, a unique time referred to as 'the last days' (2 Timothy 3:1).

Let me say one thing before I go further. God is not going to destroy the world. He is not going to destroy humankind. He is going to redeem the world and humankind along with it. Even humankind will not be permitted to destroy the world, though we are making a very good job of it at the moment.

God gave the earth to humankind to look after it, to manage it, just like He placed Adam and his wife, Eve, in the Garden of Eden to manage it, to look after it, to tend and care for it. Adam and Eve failed in their God-given mission. We've failed in ours, too. Many of Jesus' parables were about Him being the real owner, and us being the caretakers and the tenants. I've spoken several times about this in our church under the heading of 'Owners or Stewards', the point here being very clear in that He expects us to look after it with diligence, with justice, mercy and righteousness. But we could only ever do that if we continued in constant, intimate, close relationship with Him, the rightful owner. Instead of managing with wisdom, justice, grace and humility, we've rejected God, and we've led instead with pride, conceit, hubris, foolishness, injustice, selfishness, greed and unrighteousness. We've also done it in such a way that we've forgotten a cardinal truth. The owner, the Lord God Himself, is coming back!

Let's look at one of the parables Jesus spoke about.

> Then He began to speak to them in parables: 'A man planted a vineyard and set a hedge around it, dug a place for the wine vat and built a tower. And he leased it to vinedressers and went into a far country. Now at vintage-time he sent a servant to the vinedressers, that he might receive some of the fruit of the

> vineyard from the vinedressers. And they took him and beat him and sent him away empty-handed. Again he sent them another servant, and at him they threw stones, wounded him in the head, and sent him away shamefully treated. And again he sent another, and him they killed; and many others, beating some and killing some. Therefore still having one son, his beloved, he also sent him to them last, saying, "They will respect my son." But those vinedressers said among themselves, "This is the heir. Come, let us kill him, and the inheritance will be ours." So they took him and killed him and cast him out of the vineyard. Therefore what will the owner of the vineyard do? *He will come and destroy the vinedressers, and give the vineyard to others.*'
> (Mark 12:1-9, my italics)

Jesus sums up the present-day situation perfectly. The Lord God is the owner. We are the tenants. Our job is to look after what is His, until He returns. It isn't difficult to see the meaning of this parable. Jesus is, of course, referring to His Father as the owner, His servants (the prophets) sent through the ages who the tenants killed and rejected. Finally God sends His only Son, whom they also murder.

In another parable, the well-known parable of the talents, lies another example of pretty much the same truth. This time it's not grapes but money. God, the Master, gives finances to three people. He makes it clear that He expects them to manage the funds until He comes back.

> For the kingdom of heaven is like a man traveling to a far country, who called his own servants and delivered his goods to them. And to one he gave five talents, to another two, and to another one, to each according to his own ability; and immediately he went on a journey. Then he who had received

> the five talents went and traded with them, and made another five talents. And likewise he who had received two gained two more also. But he who had received one went and dug in the ground, and hid his lord's money. After a long time the lord of those servants came and settled accounts with them.
> (Matthew 25:14-30)

The message is one of responsible management. Jesus taught us to lead with integrity, mercy and humility. He epitomised this through His own lifestyle, even though many of the disciples didn't get it.

We are now in the era known as the 'last days' and there are many characteristics of this particular era. Lawlessness, greed, materialism, leading to idolatry, violence, war, famine, earthquakes, various natural catastrophes, and even a 'falling away' from the faith (2 Thessalonians 2:3-4; see also Matthew 24; 2 Timothy 3:1-9).

This book is not intended to be a book on eschatology (doctrine of the last days), but it is impossible to exclude certain aspects that lead up to the conclusion of *Code Red*, and the whole plan of redemption. For this reason, it's important to highlight certain important aspects the Bible teaches will be signs and harbingers of things to come. In 2 Thessalonians, quoted above, Paul writes of the 'falling away'. This is also in the context of a person being 'revealed', which many believe to be the Antichrist, called here 'the son of perdition'. This occurrence fits into the framework of the last chapter in which we looked at the personal biochip we will be forced to have implanted into our bodies.

Another of the signs of the end times is that which Peter refers to:

> knowing this first: that scoffers will come in the last days, walking according to their own lusts, and saying, 'Where is the promise of His coming? For since the fathers fell asleep, all things continue as they were from the beginning of creation.'
> (2 Peter 3:3-4)

One of the signs of the end of this present age is the falling away and the scepticism that follows. We are, I suggest to you, in that era right now. The time has been long, for sure, but this was even alluded to in the parable of the talents: 'After a long time the lord of those servants came and settled accounts with them.' So, the Bible shows this is not a short time, but a long time. Approximately 2,000 years have passed since this prophecy was written, but the time elapsed does not invalidate its authenticity. This is the only age in which all of the pieces are starting to fit. The parables of Jesus point to His return. The signs of the times point to His return. Eventually there will come a time when Christ will return to the earth.

No one, not a single person, knows exactly when this will be. The eschatological prophecies make it clear that He will come suddenly, and it will be unexpected and unanticipated by the majority of people (see 1 Thessalonians 5:2; 2 Peter 3:10). Jesus Himself taught that it will catch many by surprise. The majority will not be ready:

> Immediately after the tribulation of those days the sun will be darkened, and the moon will not give its light; the stars will fall from heaven, and the powers of the heavens will be shaken. Then the sign of the Son of Man will appear in heaven, and then all the tribes of the earth will mourn, and they will see the Son of Man coming on the clouds of heaven with power and great glory.
> (Matthew 24:29-30)

This is strikingly similar to the apostle John's writings in the book of Revelation:

> Behold, He is coming with clouds, and every eye will see Him, even they who pierced Him. And all the tribes of the earth will mourn because of Him. Even so, Amen.
> (Revelation 1:7)

Just stop and consider this for a moment: 'every eye will see Him'. When you think of the time this prophecy was written, in about AD60, the idea, the very concept, of the whole world, 'every eye' being able to see the returning Jesus was not remotely possible and pretty much unthinkable. Yet here we have John making this bold claim, before television, before satellites were strategically placed to make this possible by social media and various other platforms. Only in these days, the last days, is this anything like possible. With the advent of social media platforms, now we're almost getting the news before it happens!

Now we will start our countdown to the 'end of days'. We will look at some of the things that are going to happen on the earth before the end of the world as we know it.

21. The Final Countdown

We will now look at just a few of the more significant points of the book of Revelation. It has always been a fascinating book, and one that eludes many. Quite a few people stay clear of it, because of the regular use of typology and imagery. Sometimes it is difficult to separate the metaphors and types from actual events and occurrences. But it's worthy in our subject context to visit one or two of the more relevant prophecies.

The book begins prophetically with the image of four horsemen commonly known as the riders of the apocalypse. In Revelation 6:1-8 we see the order of the first rider through to the fourth. The first, on a white horse, brings peace. But it is a false peace. It almost immediately gives way to the second rider, who rides a red horse. The colour is obvious in its relevance, as it speaks of war and bloodshed. It's very interesting that it follows on from peace. Following on from this is a black horse. Here is a great famine, as one might expect following war. Whether this is a worldwide famine, we can only speculate. The last horse is a pale horse, which symbolises sickness and disease. Here's where it gets very poignant.

The fourth rider is incredibly destructive and wreaks havoc upon the earth. He is given a name, unlike the other riders. His name is Death, and he is given power to destroy one-quarter of the population either by sword (warfare), hunger (famine), death (probably disease), and 'by the beasts of the earth' (verse 8). What 'the beasts of the earth' refers to is a complete mystery as there is nothing I could think of that would be so destructive or plenteous in the animal kingdom as to fulfil this. However, several Bible commentaries state that 'the beasts of the earth' is a euphemism for brutal and sadistic people, that is: beastly. That would certainly make more sense to me. All the above happens as the 'fourth seal' is opened (verse 7). A quarter of the world's population would presently be about 1.95 billion people.

The world's population has grown rapidly over the last 160 years. Apparently, it took approximately 1,800 years for the world's population to reach approximately 1 billion. Then from 1800 to 2020, in 220 years the world has grown by 6.8 billion, to reach a present 7.8 billion. We are on target to reach nearly 9 billion by 2030 and at least 11 maybe 12 billion by 2050. Many economists believe this is totally unsustainable;[60] will it ever happen? The current coronavirus pandemic sweeping the world may in the end take out a million or more people, but nothing like what these numbers are suggesting in the book of Revelation. Nevertheless, the rapid rise in population growth may create the perfect landscape for apocalyptic decimation.

The next apocalyptic nightmare in the book of Revelation is a cosmic one. Under the sixth seal, there is a huge earthquake. It may well be that this is triggered by a meteor crashing to the earth, and causing huge seismic destruction, but there is no doubt this is so violent it shakes the earth to its foundations and marks the beginning of the end (Revelation 6:12-17).

There is an interlude after the sixth seal and preceding the seventh seal being opened. The opening of the seventh seal in heaven leads into seven more terrifying judgements to be unleashed upon the earth.

The chronology of the apocalypse is very difficult to ascertain. If we follow the opening of the seven seals until the sounding of the seven trumpets, that sits alright. It gets a little harder, then, to place the most terrifying of all judgements unleashed upon the earth, that of the seven bowls. The seven seals I would describe as awful, the seven trumpets as terrifying, but the seven bowls are just beyond description – they go beyond anything you could imagine. Also, it

60. Jordan Rangers www.vox.com Earth's population trend explained. By Kelsey Piper August 20, 2019.

seems the seven bowls are poured out within a relatively short space of time.

So, the seventh seal is opened and the first trumpet sounds.

The seven trumpets

The first trumpet (Revelation 8:7). The destruction of a third of trees and grass is the first thing that happens. Vegetation is scorched. In Australia, starting in June 2019, the worst bushfires on record hit the continent. By September, new out of control fires ravaged the landscape. These fires worsened significantly in November 2019. I remember distinctly leading our congregation in prayers for rain, along with many thousands of churches and hundreds of thousands of Christians worldwide. Heavy rain came in the afternoon of our prayer time, and I have the evidence on my phone as we thanked God together for His mercy. This rain enabled firefighters to get some of the blaze under control. However, hotter temperatures followed later after this respite, and high winds escalated the crisis. The first weekend of February, the fires started to rage again, and more fires sprang up synonymously. Again prayers went up. In mid-February an extremely heavy amount of rainfall allowed firefighters to curtail these raging furnaces. Many lives were lost, and more than 100,000 sheep died and 25,000 livestock too. This trumpet judgement puts this tragic event into perspective. *This is on a much larger scale.*[61]

The second trumpet (Revelation 8:8-9). The second trumpet sounds, and it features a huge meteorite hurled into the sea. A third of the sea becomes like blood and a third of sea life is destroyed. A third of ships are also destroyed. The 'third' becomes a repetitive theme throughout the apocalypse.

61. Information taken from www.disasterphilanthropy.org; www.weforum.org; www.metro.co.uk (accessed 7.6.20).

The third trumpet (Revelation 8:10-11). This time some kind of asteroid or again meteor hits the rivers and sources of them. It's given a name, 'Wormwood', because it is bitter. The Greek word is '*apsinthos*' and implies a bitter or even toxic plant. One-third of the rivers become bitter, and many people die from drinking from them.

The fourth trumpet (Revelation 8:12-13). This trumpet affects the sun, moon and stars. A third of these planetary bodies do not give their light, resulting in a third of the day being in darkness. A warning from the angels in heaven is then given about the next three trumpets.

The fifth trumpet (Revelation 9:1-12). This is where things start to become terrifying. The bottomless pit is opened. Several versions use the term 'abyss' (e.g. NIV, 'Abyss'). There are several words in the Greek for the underworld. Hades, the grave, hell are the most common. There is a word in the Greek called 'Tartarus' which does not refer simply to Hades, the grave, or even hell. It refers to the place where the fallen angels are kept chained until this moment in time (2 Peter 2:4).

Hopefully, now you'll begin to see just how important our referencing has been. Do you remember when we spoke of Jesus about to cast out the Nephilim spirits (demons) out of Legion earlier? They begged Jesus not to send them into 'the abyss' (Luke 8:31). Out of this abyss came creatures like 'locusts' with stings like 'scorpions'. Truly horrific!

What is really interesting here is the timeframe these beings are given to torment humankind upon the earth. Five months! I'm emphasising this so that you can see the specific times the scripture is giving us. Also, that these beings are not allowed to take life, but to 'torment' it. These last three trumpet blasts are referred to as the 'three woes'. This is the first.

The sixth trumpet (and second woe – Revelation 13:9-21). The release of the four imprisoned angels at the river Euphrates. It is possible that somewhere in this vicinity is a doorway into the spirit dimension. Strangely enough, it is not that far from Eden, and one of the rivers flowing out from the Garden of Eden was the Euphrates (Genesis 2:14).

These four angels release 'fire, smoke, and brimstone'. The results are catastrophic. One-third of the global population is killed by the advent of these four angels upon the earth. Taking into consideration all the preceding calamities and plagues, famines and a fourth (one-quarter) of the population being destroyed under the fourth seal (approximately 1.95 billion) add to this the lives lost in the preceding and following plagues and judgements (500 million), this leaves about 5.35 billion upon the face of the earth. A fourth or quarter of this total to be killed under the sixth trumpet leaves only 4 billion people on the face of the earth! We started off with a population of 7.8 billion this is virtually halved by the apocalypse with all its terror and horror.

The seventh trumpet (Revelation 11:15-19). This seems to signify the end of the age, though somewhere, somehow, the seven bowls of wrath will be poured out.

The writer of the Revelation is not concerned with chronology so much as descriptiveness. He uses whatever language he can to describe the unique and mind-blowing scenes he witnesses in his vision. For the next few chapters, he seems to go back and record other events culminating in the destruction of 'the beast' and 'false prophet' (Revelation 19:20), characters that personify Satan in his last-ditch attempts to try to get the world to worship him by force and falsehood. John, however, picks up on the most severe of all the judgements that comes in the form of the 'seven bowls of God's wrath' (Acts 16:1, NIV). They appear to come right at the end of the period of great tribulation that Jesus Himself referred to in Matthew 24:21, and seem to come in quick succession.

The seven bowls

The first bowl (Revelation 16:2). 'Malignant' (Amplified Version) sores come upon people. Possibly in the form of melanomas and are likely to be cancerous. Truly shocking and horrific.

The second bowl (Revelation 16:3). The bowl is poured into the sea. The sea then congeals like a dead man's blood. *Everything* living in the sea dies!

The third bowl (Revelation 16:4). This bowl is poured into the freshwater courses, including their sources (springs). I'm assuming that as in the second bowl, all life dies within.

The fourth bowl (Revelation 16:8-9) is poured out upon the sun. It causes humankind to be scorched with a great heat.

The fifth bowl (Revelation 16:10). This is directed upon 'the beast' and his kingdom. It seems darkness comes upon them. Whether this is a literal, physical darkness, one cannot say for sure, but there is an allusion in the previous verses in the fourth bowl to 'plagues' (verse 9). When we read about the plagues upon Israel, darkness was certainly one of the plagues (Exodus 10:21), as were sores (Exodus 9:10) and water becoming like blood (Exodus 7:20).

The sixth bowl (Revelation 16:12-14). This bowl is poured out upon the river Euphrates. It dries the river up to prepare the way for the 'kings [rulers] of the east'. This seems to preclude the infamous battle of Armageddon, which appears to be on the outskirts of Jerusalem. (Some believe it to be in the Jezreel Valley, which is a large triangular tract of land perfect for a large military campaign. Others believe it to refer to the Valley of Megiddo on the outskirts of Jerusalem, which was known to be a place of slaughter and the site where many idolatrous kings sacrificed their sons and daughter to the Nephilim gods of Remphan and Molech, amongst other pseudo-deities.)

The seventh bowl (Revelation 16:17-21). A huge earthquake hits the city of Jerusalem. It splits the city into three parts. Enormous hailstones come crashing down from heaven. The angel upon pouring their bowl of wrath out says, 'It is done' (verse 17) – similar, surely, to Christ's words upon the cross: 'It is finished' (John 19:30) – '*tetelestai*' in Greek: it is accomplished! From this moment, and according to the following chapters, this sees Christ's return to the earth and is the same event as that which is outlined in Zechariah's prophecy (Zechariah 14:4), and by Luke in Acts 1:11.

In the Zechariah prophecy, it says that the Mount of Olives splits in two, whilst the event in Revelation says the city splits into three. I see no problem here. The Mount of Olives splits in two. Zechariah says it will split from 'east to west', meaning it will probably go straight through the eastern gate (in itself a prophecy that even Messianic Jews believe will happen one day soon).[62] This eastern gate has been sealed until Messiah comes. The fissure will go right through the gate, fulfilling the prophecy, through the Temple Mount, through the Holy of Holies, towards the Mediterranean Sea, thereby dividing the north of the city from the south. Further fracturing would probably

62. 'What is the significance of the Eastern Gate of Jerusalem?' www.gotquestions.org (accessed 4.3.20). www.bible-history.com is a good site to visit.

take place from the city to the north or the city to the south, literally leaving the city in three distinct parts.

Acts 1:11 is the record of Jesus' ascension into heaven. Guess where It took place? On the Mount of Olives. The important bit is the message of the angels. Exactly as you see Him go, He will come back. What amazing symmetry here. He's coming back physically, literally, actually and really!

I realise that these last two chapters paint a very bleak picture of the future of our world and its inhabitants, *but we have been warned.* We have been warned so that we may be able to escape this forthcoming apocalyptic nightmare.

Paul said, 'God did not appoint us to wrath, but to obtain salvation through our Lord Jesus Christ' (1 Thessalonians 5:9). *There is a way of escape.* It is by accepting the message of salvation through the cross of Jesus Christ.

At the beginning of the book, I spent some time emphasising that Noah was ordered to build an ark, a huge boat that would go on to rescue those who would hear the message of salvation. That message included warnings of 'things not yet seen' by humanity at that time (Hebrews 11:7). Noah preached for many years. No one paid much attention to him. The rain surely came, and only eight people were saved from sudden catastrophic destruction. As someone once pointed out, 'It wasn't raining when Noah built the ark.'[63]

Today, little has changed. Many are preaching the same message about things coming upon the planet that we have never seen. Many of these things I've written about right here. But it's all there in the Bible and I challenge you to go check it out.

In the next chapter I will share with you in more detail the way of escape. The way out! I ask you to look around at our world today.

63. Source unknown, although attributed to author, political commentator and financial advisor Howard Ruff.

Watch, observe. We can often predict the weather reasonably well, but we can't discern the times in which we're living. Most people know 'the end is coming' but they don't understand how, why or when. There is a bigger plan, that of redemption.

On bringing this chapter to a close, I'd ask you to do the same thing as Noah asked the people of his day. 'Get into the ark, before it's too late!'

22. Your Seat Has Been Reserved

Imagine, for the moment, the world was on fire. Then Elon Musk or Richard Branson calls you personally to tell you, 'Hey, listen! I've got a seat for you and your family to come on our space shuttle to Cenador, the new planet we found that's even better, bigger and cleaner than earth.' You'd say, 'Erm… OK, but how much?' You would probably be thinking it's at least a million pounds a ticket. Then they say, 'Actually, it's free, because someone paid for the seats. All you need to do is say yes, accept them and we'll do the rest.' There is no way you would refuse. You'd look at the burning planet and pack your bags as soon as possible (in case someone changed their mind). Guess what? The planet is beginning to burn up. We are on an irrecoverable, irreversible spiral moving towards the end time apocalypse described in this book. So it's time to book your seat!

The most common statement you'll hear from people concerning God, is: 'If God is a God of love, why would He put His creation through this kind of nightmare? Surely He would not allow this to happen?' For sure, God is full of love and mercy. He does not want anyone to be lost. Eternity awaits us all. I said earlier in the book, a spirit does not die. Well, you and I have a spirit. This body is just a shell. It will pass away, with 100 per cent certainty. But our spirit will continue to live forever. That's why God sent His Son, Jesus, into this world.

> For God so loved the world that He gave His only begotten Son, that whoever believes in Him should not perish but have everlasting life.
> (John 3:16)

We are told also that 'there will be a resurrection of … both … the just and the unjust' (Acts 24:15). There is no doubt about that. The fact that Christ died for us all, each and every one of us, is our way of escape. At the back of *Code Red* I've written a little prayer that can start a whole new beginning in your life. You will also find an address so you can contact me if you need any further help. Praying this prayer from the heart will be like booking your seat to eternity, ready for God's exit strategy.

God's exit strategy

The Bible is full of hope and positivity for those who accept God's plan of redemption. Here I'm going to share a most remarkable miracle that is going to happen soon. Many of you will not have heard of the Rapture of the Church. This is the name given amongst Christians for the 'catching away' of those who love God and have accepted His free gift of salvation. *God will literally airlift His people from the earth,* so they escape the awful judgements predetermined to happen upon the earth. Jesus Himself alluded to it when He taught His disciples on the Mount of Olives:

> Then two men will be in the field: one will be taken and the other left. Two women will be grinding at the mill: one will be taken and the other left. Watch therefore, for you do not know what hour your Lord is coming.
> (Matthew 24:40-42)

The message is clear and very poignant. Jesus is challenging His disciples to be ready so they are not left behind. Paul also reminds us:

> But concerning the times and the seasons, brethren, you have no need that I should write to you. For you yourselves

> know perfectly that the day of the Lord so *comes as a thief in the night.* For when they say, 'Peace and safety!' then sudden destruction comes upon them, as labor pains upon a pregnant woman. And they shall not escape. But you, brethren, are not in darkness, *so that this Day should overtake you as a thief.*
> (1 Thessalonians 5:1-4, my italics)

The metaphor of the thief is not only used by Paul, but by Peter too:

> But the day of the Lord will *come as a thief in the night*, in which the heavens will pass away with a great noise, and the elements will melt with fervent heat; both the earth and the works that are in it will be burned up.
> (2 Peter 3:10, my italics)

Paul teaches us in more detail on this incredible and momentous occasion.

> Behold, I tell you a mystery: We shall not all sleep, but we shall all be changed – in a moment, in the twinkling of an eye, at the last trumpet. For the trumpet will sound, and the dead will be raised incorruptible, and we shall be changed.
> (1 Corinthians 15:51-52)

The phrase 'We shall not all sleep' refers to those who Christians who have died. Something the Bible often refers to as sleep: looking towards the resurrection of their bodies to eternal life. But we shall be changed; 'in a moment', in the 'twinkling of an eye'! This is known to Bible students and scholars as the 'translation of the saints', that is, the change from terrestrial to celestial bodies in the blink of an eye. Paul sums it up even more clearly in his letter to the Thessalonians:

> For this we say to you by the word of the Lord, that we who are alive and remain until the coming of the Lord will by no means precede those who are asleep. For the Lord Himself will descend from heaven with a shout, with the voice of an archangel, and with the trumpet of God. And the dead in Christ will rise first. Then we who are alive and remain shall be caught up together with them in the clouds to meet the Lord in the air. And thus we shall always be with the Lord. Therefore comfort one another with these words.
> (1 Thessalonians 4:15-18)

So in these verses of Scripture is both resurrection (of those who died/sleep in faith) and translation to those who remain. This is not the Second Coming of Christ to the earth when every eye shall see Him (Acts 1:11).

Coming like a thief means that people will not see Him coming. Many will wake up in the morning, so to speak, and find many people have gone. The figure of the 'thief' is meant to illustrate the stealth with which the Lord will come. After this, the way is open for all the judgements, plagues, wars, wrath and tribulation to be unleashed upon the earth, following which the visible, physical return of the Lord will occur.

I realise that this will seem unbelievable, far-fetched and even fanciful to many reading this book, but it has always been taught and preached down through all the ages until this present day. Everything, of course, depends on whether we believe in the Bible as being God's supreme Word or not. Who would have thought that we would have been in lockdown for months worldwide through a pandemic known as the coronavirus? Who could have foreseen what 2020 would bring? Remember, Jesus spoke of such things.

> Then Jesus told them, 'Nation will rise against nation and kingdom against kingdom. There will be violent earthquakes, and in various places famines and [deadly and devastating] pestilences (plagues, epidemics); and there will be terrible sights and great signs from heaven.
> (Luke 21:10-11, Amplified Version)

In 2020 we entered a whole new era that I believe will introduce a whole new series of events that will be 'signs' to help us know that we need God's intervention in our lives. Who would've thought that we would have witnessed the brutal barbarity of ISIS? Who'd have ever expected to be seeing men and women and even children crucified, live beheadings, people thrown off buildings and burned alive? Hundreds of people are being butchered and senselessly murdered every week, just because they're Christians, in Nigeria. Chinese Christians are being arrested just for watching online Christian church services. Eritrean pastors are beaten, imprisoned and tortured, their churches razed to the ground.[64]

I hope and pray *Code Red* at least begins to open your eyes to a much bigger picture than you ever imagined before. I hope this book helps to fill many blanks in for you, regarding that bigger picture. It is like one humongous jigsaw puzzle. All the pieces fit, but only one Person knows exactly how, where and when they will be fitted in and pieced together. That is the Lord God Almighty Himself.

We're nearing our conclusion now, but some of the final pieces can be seen to fit into the numerous gaps that still remain.

---

64. Doug Bandow, 'A New Ranking of Nations Where Christians are Persecuted Most', 28 January 2020, www.nationalreview.com; Nigeria, www.opendoorsuk.org; also Emeka Umeagbalasi, www.genocidewatch.com, 'Nigeria is a Killing Field of Defenceless Christians', 13 April 2020 (accessed 7.6.20).

23. So What Happens Next?

At the end of this age, a new era will begin; the age we are now in will culminate with one huge global conflict called Armageddon. The nations will converge upon Jerusalem. Just at that time, the prophecies I mentioned earlier, when we spoke of Zechariah, Luke and Peter, Paul and Jesus Himself will be fulfilled. Satan will be put in chains, along with his kingdom and all the Nephilim spirit beings in his kingdom; eventually, they will all be cast into the lake of fire (Revelation 20:1-3).

A new age will then begin. This age is often referred to as 'the Millennium' because of its duration. Many evangelicals do not believe in this train of thought, even though it is clearly predicted and timeframed in the Scripture. There has yet to be a plausible argument against it, in my opinion, and certainly nothing else fits the biblical prophecies referring to this 'golden age' as it's also been referred to in the past. Isaiah 11:6-9 quite obviously refers to an age the like of which we've never seen.

Here are some more truths that will help to fill in the blanks to the bigger picture. The abyss that we saw earlier, from which the imprisoned fallen angels were loosed, is now to be the prison of Satan and all his cohorts. They will be chained for 1,000 years, heralding a new age of time without his direct influence upon the earth.

This new epoch of time has several characteristics that make it unique and totally different to all that has been before us, certainly since Eden. Whether the new world along with the new heavens is created before the Millennium of after it, is a point of debate. It appears to be just after the Millennium that a new heaven and a new earth are created (Revelation 21:1).

1. Longevity of age is restored.

    No more shall an infant from there live but a few days,
    Nor an old man who has not fulfilled his days;
    For the child shall die one hundred years old,
    But the sinner being one hundred years old shall be accursed.
    (Isaiah 65:20)

2. Dangerous animals become docile.

    The wolf also shall dwell with the lamb,
    The leopard shall lie down with the young goat,
    The calf and the young lion and the fatling together;
    And a little child shall lead them.
    (Isaiah 11:6)

3. There will be no sorrow.

    The voice of weeping shall no longer be heard in her,
    Nor the voice of crying.
    (Isaiah 65:19)

4. Satan and his kingdom will be absent.

    The devil, who deceived them, was cast into the lake of fire and brimstone where the beast and the false prophet are. And they will be tormented day and night forever and ever.
    (Revelation 20:10)

5. All the people of the world will come to worship God.

> And it shall come to pass
> That from one New Moon to another,
> And from one Sabbath to another,
> All flesh shall come to worship before Me,' says the LORD.
> (Isaiah 66:23)

This 'golden age', however, will not last. The problem of sin still being in the genes of the human race will eventually resurface. A population of some 2-2.5 billion left upon the earth will look to rebuild and restore a largely decimated world; though regeneration will take place, it is not going to last.

At the end of the 1,000 years, Satan and his armies are loosed upon the earth as a test of allegiance to the people of the world. Many will again be turned by his allure, and he manages to muster a great and mighty army to attack the Lord God in Jerusalem again. This will, however, lead to the final conflict and he will be given a bruising lesson. The Lord God then takes Satan, along with all his army, his hordes of fallen angels and Nephilim spirits, and casts him into the 'lake of fire' (sulphur) where, says the scripture, this shall be a place of burning for ever and ever (Revelation 20:7-10). There shall be no more release, no mercy shall be shown to Satan and his emissaries. At this point we enter the second resurrection. That is, the souls of all who have died in disbelief and outside of faith shall be raised to life physically, in order to face the judgement of God.

What is known as the Great White Throne judgement has at last come (Revelation 20:11-15). The first resurrection is the resurrection of all those who have died in faith in Christ Jesus. This event precedes the Great White Throne judgement. The first resurrection is also an event in several stages or phases. The first phase was at Christ's resurrection when He became 'the firstfruits from among the dead' (1 Corinthians 15:20), and the second phrase, what occurs at His coming for His Church, the Rapture, described in 1 Thessalonians 4:15-20.

Then, there is another part of the first resurrection, which is basically those who refuse the mark of the beast in the end times after the Rapture (Revelation 20:4-5).

So, once this is completed at the end of the age, there is no more resurrection until after the Millennium. It appears if all those with faith who are born in the period of the Millennium will last the duration of it, physically. There may even be healing and the eradication of sickness during the 1,000-year reign. Afterwards, however, the end-time judgement will come, and a new world will be created along with a new heaven (sky above).

> Blessed and holy is he who has part in the first resurrection. Over such the second death has no power, but they shall be priests of God and of Christ, and shall reign with Him a thousand years.
> (Revelation 20:6)

Those of us who have been raised to life in the first resurrection will have a new body that is totally different from our existing terrestrial body. We will have a celestial body.

> For our citizenship is in heaven, from which we also eagerly wait for the Savior, the Lord Jesus Christ, who will transform our lowly body that it may be conformed to His glorious body, according to the working by which He is able even to subdue all things to Himself.
> (Philippians 3:20-21)

This celestial body is exactly like the prototype, Christ's resurrected body, which was physical (John 20:27) but it is also a spirit body, a body that is no longer bound by the natural physical limitations of the dimension we live in today. Therefore, once we have been raised to eternal life, we will be able to materialise and dematerialise at will. Furthermore, we will have roles and tasks to do, as the Lord Himself alluded to so many times.[65]

As regards heaven, it is a very real place. It is material, celestial and spiritual. Those who die in faith will probably be able to move between worlds with ease – the new world, for instance, and that of heaven as in God's own throne room and His dwelling place. And so the plan of redemption is completed in Christ Jesus. He had the first word back in the beginning (Genesis 1:1) and He will also have the last word. He is, of course, 'the Alpha and Omega, the Beginning and the End' (Revelation 22:13).

Thank you so much for reading *Code Red.* I appreciate you spending your time when you have so many alternative choices. Though you may not agree with many things I've said, the most important message within these chapters is that God's Son, Jesus, came to redeem (buy back) every one of us. Not just in a general sense, but personally too. You are the reason He came. You are the reason why He died, and You are the reason why He's coming back again.

I would dearly love you to make sure *you take your place* in God's great plan of redemption, by making sure you've given your life to Him, through His Son, Jesus. He alone died for us, *so that we could be forgiven and have a new life and a future hope after this life.* If you haven't done that yet, I would ask you to pray the prayer at the end of this book. By all means cut it out and keep it as a reminder that you've booked your place in eternity.

---

65. Luke 19:15-19; Luke 22:30; 1 Corinthians 6:3; Revelation 22:3.

I hope to meet you one day. If not in this life, in the one that is far better and sweeter, the one that is to follow.

God bless.

Not the end, but a new beginning!

My Personal Prayer

Dear Lord,

I come to you today, realising and accepting the fact that You sent Your Son to this earth to die for me, so I could be forgiven and set free from sin's power and its grip on me.

I confess my sin and ask you to forgive me for all my wrongdoings. Please accept me as a child of God from this day forward. Help me to trust in You and help me to start living my new life for You and in the power of Your Holy Spirit. Give me strength to live for You and help me find my purpose for living in Your kingdom.

Thank you for my new life. Help me to now live in appreciation and praise for the rest of my days here on earth, until I see You face to face.

Amen.

If you prayed that prayer and you need further help and direction, please feel free to write to me personally at:

The Lighthouse Church Manchester UK
Unit 12, Centenary Park
Coronet Way,
Eccles
Manchester
M50 1RE

I promise I will reply personally to all who write to me.

Yours in Him,

Paul Hallam (Pastor)